TEACHING KIDS TO READ

TEACHING KIDS TO READ

Embracing Guided Reading in Primary School Classrooms

GAIL SAUNDERS-SMITH

Skyhorse Publishing

Skyhorse Publishing books may be purchased in bulk at special discounts for sales promotion, corporate gifts, fund-raising, or educational purposes. Special editions can also be created to specifications. For details, contact the Special Sales Department, Skyhorse Publishing, 307 West 36th Street, 11th Floor, New York, NY 10018 or info@skyhorsepublishing.com.

Skyhorse® and Skyhorse Publishing® are registered trademarks of Skyhorse Publishing, Inc.®, a Delaware corporation.

Visit our website at www.skyhorsepublishing.com.

10 9 8 7 6 5 4 3 2 1

Library of Congress Cataloging-in-Publication Data is available on file.

Cover design by David Ter-Avanesyan
Cover photo: Shutterstock

Print ISBN: 978-1-5107-6924-3
Ebook ISBN: 978-1-5107-7016-4

Printed in China

Contents

Acknowledgments

"As humans, we learn from each other." That was the first sentence in the first edition of this book, and it remains the first sentence in this edition because it is true. The older I get, the truer the phrase "lifelong learner" becomes. Just when we think we know it all, something else comes along to shift our understanding. I guess that's why the species has continued—you learn something new every day. As with the first edition, this book represents what I have continued to learn from other people. Now is my chance to say thank you for all that you have helped me learn.

This book could not have been written without administrators, teachers, and colleagues who invited me into their districts and classrooms and who welcomed me into their conversations. Thanks continue to go to all those who made the first edition possible and to those who continued my learning, including: Debbie Hagg of Youngstown City Schools; Kathie Carlile and the teachers and children at E. J. Blott Elementary in Liberty, Ohio; the teachers and children in Hudson, Ohio schools; and the teachers and children at Kleckner Elementary in Green, Ohio. I thank the undergraduates in the Early Childhood Department at the Beeghly College of Education at Youngstown State University for giving me reason to rethink everything I thought I knew. I thank the following people who have been instrumental in continuing the path that has become my professional life: Phil Ginnetti, Mary Lou DiPillo, Dora Bailey, Gay Su Pinnell, and Marie Clay.

Sincere thanks for kind encouragement, knowledgable guidance, and enduring patience go to Susan Jarvis, Joanna Coelho, Amy Schroller, and Jessica Alan at Corwin.

Heartfelt thanks go to the memories of my mother and father, Ruth and John Saunders, who together made reading and writing a natural, integral part of our lives; and to the memory of my husband, Chuck Smith, who took care of everyone and everything. Thank you, thank you, thank you!

Without each of you, what is would not be.

Additionally, the publisher would like to acknowledge the following peer reviewer for her editorial insight and guidance:

Deb Bible, NBCT
Literacy Teacher and Consultant
Dundee Highlands School
West Dundee, IL

About the Author

**Gail Saunders-Smith** is an assistant professor of literacy in the Beeghly College of Education at Youngstown State University. She is a former primary-level classroom teacher and Reading Recovery® teacher leader. She continued to work with children and teachers when she served eight school districts as Reading/Language Arts K–12 Supervisor and Coordinator of State and Federal Programs and as independent national staff developer.

Much in demand as a lively and well-informed presenter, she has given workshops across the United States and Canada on all aspects of literacy development. Gail has visited schools in Great Britain, New Zealand, Australia, and Russia.

Gail has published a number of teacher support materials. She has also published more than 46 nonfiction little books and five big books for emergent readers, including selections that are part of the Pair-It Books series and others as part of the Pebble Books series. Gail is a consulting editor for Red Brick Learning, an imprint of Capstone Press. In addition, she has published articles on early literacy development in a number of journals.

Gail holds a BS and an MA in early childhood education, an MS in administration and supervision, and a PhD in early literacy development. She describes herself as a reader, writer, teacher, and student.

Introduction

So, what's new? Well, as an educational society, we now have scientific evidence—thanks to the neuroscientists—that new knowledge does attach to existing knowledge: Vygotsky was right! We are realizing more and more that as the planet continues to shrink, educators have a responsibility to differentiate more than ever before. The need to differentiate has pervaded cultural (including language, religion, traditions, and beliefs), cognitive, physical, psychosocial, and other aspects of classroom life. This edition attempts to address the constructivist nature of learning and the increasing need to differentiate. This edition represents the continued thinking about and working with children in learning how to read. Experience shapes and reshapes what we once thought we knew. The changes in my understandings, my increased awareness and understanding, are documented here. The book remains a practitioner's guide to teaching children how to read.

What is the same? Well, we continue to read and to teach children to read. Educators—most of us, anyway—read everything from professional books and journals to those quality trashy novels. Ah, the trashy novel. . . . The question remains the same: How did we get this way? What happened that made us such consumers of print? More important, how do we help our students to become such readers?

HOW IT HAPPENED

The Introduction to the first edition of this book invited you, the reader, to think back to how you learned to read. How old were you? Was it in school or out of school? Who was involved? What kinds of things do you remember reading? How did you feel about reading and being a reader? Was it pleasant or frustrating?

I admitted that I could not remember exactly how or at what point reading began for me. I shared a few stories of reading at home, being read to as a child, and just sort of *learning* how to read without being *taught* to read. As I look back on this now, I realize that my brother and I lived in an environment where reading happened all around us, all the time. I suppose you could say he and I were immersed in a literate environment. We saw reading happening as we watched our parents read newspapers and books. We were read to in the evenings before bed and on the front porch in the summer. We got books from the library every Saturday and read them over and over again, whether we could read them or not. I suppose it is true: you learn what you live, and we lived reading. No wonder we learned to read before we were taught to read.

I also admitted to being a middle-group student, and the dilemma it posed my parents. It was all the fault of Dick and Jane et al.: I now realize that part of the problem was that my schema for family did not match the family in the Dick and Jane house. While my father did go to work in a white shirt and tie and dress trousers, my mother wore neither pearls nor heels at home. We had neither cat nor dog—nor, indeed, a baby sister. And the Zeke in our lives was the man who lived alone in the house on the corner with the high grass to whom we were told not to speak.

The other issue causing my middle-group placement was the fact that my experience with text did not match the text provided in the Dick and Jane books. See, the books I was used to seeing had multiple lines of text, full sentences that sounded like talking. The first-grade Dick and Jane books of the forties and fifties had few words, sometimes only one or two, on a page. This confounded and confused me, because I could not make meaning from just "Look!" I looked like a slow reader because, in my mind, I was trying to fill in the gaps of plot and character interplay that the minimal words caused. I was indeed the daydreamer the teachers said I was.

My third admission concerned a semantic issue—the meaning of "Father." You see, I went to Catholic school, and the man called "Father" was the priest. The Father I knew wore only a black suit with a black shirt and a thin white collar around his neck, and he lived alone in the rectory next to the church. At six years of age, I was morally conflicted when introduced to a different "Father," one who wore a brown suit and lived in a house with some woman and her kids. (This was before I knew about Episcopalians.)

So, this book addresses the need to consider schema and to differentiate to ensure that learning occurs from the teaching we do. We'll take a look at ways that reading happens in the mind, ways to provide for awareness, direct instruction, guided practice, and independent practice at each stage of literacy development. In addition, we'll examine ways to differentiate instruction by accommodating expectations, materials, and instructional practices. I hope you enjoy, and learn from, this new edition.

HOW WE DID IT

Regardless of the methods and materials that we learned to read from and with, we turned out okay. Think about how we taught reading as teachers. I and many of my age-mates (counting the years or months to retirement, worrying about Social Security and long-term health care) have seen it all in reading instruction. So much so, we could write a book!

The small-group thing that we did early in our careers, in the sixties and seventies, wasn't so different from how we learned to read. We had the three groups and the worksheets, and we moved the kids progressively through the stories, one after another, five days on a story, then on to the next one. And you know what? Those kids learned to read! Some of them even became teachers.

Then we saw the advent, duration, and demise of whole language, whatever that was. Some of us did the literature-based thing. This was an interesting period in American education. We stopped phonicating and did the whole-word and whole-idea thing while we worked with the whole group of kids—everyone reading the same book. We selected a book not because it was within the students' zone of proximal development, or because it contained the concepts, skills, and vocabulary these students needed, or offered specific strategy use or comprehending opportunities; no, we chose a book because then we could make a quilt. That era was marked with such fascinating symbols: many of us wore denim skirts and wooden jewelry, and we placed woven baskets and wallpaper borders in our classrooms. And you know what? Most of those kids learned to read! Some of *them* even became teachers.

AND HERE WE ARE

Yep, here we are, even further along than we were ten years ago when the science of learning first peeked over the educational horizon. Many of us are still teaching reading. Granted, some of us may be looking at the golden rays of retirement, peering longingly at the enticing pink hues of reading anything we want at any time, maybe even joining a real book club. But, until that really happens, we keep showing up every day, teaching those kids who keep showing up how to read. The sobering reality is that the majority of these children we are teaching today will work in the health-care field in some capacity at some point in their lives. And they'll be taking care of us!

It seems as though we've seen it all. Guided reading is not a new concept: many districts across the United States and Canada have implemented this teaching practice to some degree. So, what's new? Actually, a lot—the science of learning has influenced the decisions we make. The changing demographics of the learning population warrant greater diversification for linguistic, cultural, cognitive, and affective concerns.

As an educational society, we have benefited from the work the scientific society has been doing. We now know so much more about brain research, language development, and literacy development in general. Teachers today are being asked to operate much more like scientists. We are being asked to make instructional decisions. We have to look at children as they operate on and with print. It has become our professional responsibility to recognize literate behaviors, analyze those behaviors, interpret them, and then use that information to form groups, select texts, and design interactions in order to provide awareness, instruction, guided practice, independent practice, and application that enable children to assimilate new information with existing information. This is sure a whole lot different from just reading the boldface print in the teacher's guide.

Four cornerstones—group formation, text selection, teaching sequence, and teacher talk—form the foundational differences between guided reading and what we used to do. The following are some of the questions that folks ask when they begin investigating the differences between what we used to do and what we are currently doing in the name of reading instruction. Perhaps some of your wonderings will be answered here. If so, great—glad to be of service. In any case, be sure to read through the rest of book. The story only gets better.

SO, TELL ME . . .

Q.   *What is the difference between ability groups and homogeneous groups? Isn't homogeneous just a new word to describe an old idea?*

A.   Nope. The differences between the two are actually small, but the impact of those differences is significant. Homogeneous groups are refinements of ability groups. That is, we sort our kids into four groups: those who process quickly or who are operating above expectations; those who process typically or who are operating as expected; those who are operating marginally at expectations or slightly below; and those who process slowly or who are operating significantly below expectations. Of course, reality dictates that any combination of group formations may result from the children who make up any classroom. In general, these groups are grossly similar; examining children's broad performances with text or their abilities forms them. Next we look again at each of those groups and determine the specifics of what skills, concepts, vocabulary, strategies, and behaviors each child knows and uses. In other words, we examine the finite nature of literacy learning and pull together those children who are most alike on this microscopic level. It is matching four, five, or six children who are so much alike that they operate as though they were one child sporting six heads. Generally, the type of analysis we do enables us to morph three ability groups into four homogeneous groups. Sometimes we have to borrow or send a child or two from or to another classroom to make a group of four to six (this is called deployment). The more alike the children in the group, the more precise the teaching can be. The more precise the teaching, the more learning occurs. (See Chapter 5 for a full discussion of grouping.)

Q.   *Do you have to do guided reading with little books, or can you do it with any kind of book, even basal programs?*

A.   Books make up one set of tools used in literacy learning. If you want to get the job done right, you need to use the right tools. Books appropriate for reading instruction provide practice with what has already been learned while offering just enough opportunities for new learning. We do guided reading with what we have, no matter what that is. Some modifications may be needed, however.

Instructional narrative texts (fiction) should be 90 to 95 percent familiar to the members of the group; expository texts (nonfiction) should be 92 to 97 percent familiar. This means the children in that group can read, figure out, and understand most of the words and the children can use most of the skills the book requires. This doesn't mean the children have read or heard the book prior to the lesson, however. Familiar texts enable children to experience a great deal of success while they work just hard enough on the few bits that offer challenges. If the book is too difficult, which is often the case with grade-level basal programs, all of the children's cognitive energy is used to figure out the words. The children become either exhausted, without enough cognitive energy to comprehend what is being read, or disinterested, without sufficient cognitive or affective stamina to keep up the fight. Books in basal programs are wonderful, with rich, vibrant stories, but this wonderfulness frequently renders them too difficult for the grade level for which they are intended. When the book is too difficult, generally the teacher must compensate in some way to bring the children to where the book is in terms of its difficulty. Frequently, that means reading it to them—which is fine, except the child who works learns, and the teacher already knows how to read. Taking children through a book that is too difficult is like me trying to squeeze into a size ten pair of jeans (I am larger than a size ten). I can let out the seams and move over the button or attach a rubber band, and then even not zip the zipper all the way. It's a lot of work and in the end the jeans just don't fit. I end up struggling, get sweaty and frustrated, and ultimately resort to eating ice cream. (Chapter 6 describes the details of analyzing texts and determining what is appropriate for which group.)

Q.   *Is there a certain way to teach a guided reading lesson? How do you handle the vocabulary, and what about the skills?*

A.   Each instructional practice has a framework of interaction, a logical progression of thinking that moves readers into and through a text. In guided reading, each of the five steps of the lesson serves a specific purpose and sets up the next step of the lesson. Vocabulary and skills are contextualized throughout the lesson so the children learn the specific words and skills in the environment in which they encounter them, and will probably encounter them in other similar situations later on. This eases the dilemma of change of state, which is learning something in one situation and not recognizing it in another.

    The first step of the lesson is setting the scene, which Madeline Hunter called the "anticipatory set." This conversation between the teacher and the children in the group orients the readers to the concept, genre, and author. In doing so, the teacher enables the children to call forth schema-relevant thoughts, experiences, language, images, and so on that the children can use to connect what the author is saying to what they already know. Setting the scene is the first whiff of comprehending; it readies the readers for what the author has to offer.

    The second step of the lesson is the book introduction. This step is most frequently used in nonfiction books that have access features such as a table of contents, index, and glossary.

    The third step of the lesson is the picture walk. The purpose of the picture walk changes depending on the instructional practice. In guided reading, for emergent and early readers, the teacher guides the children's attention through the pictures in order to alert the children to potential sources of information for strategy use. In transitional guided reading, the pictures alert the readers to the literary elements of character, setting, and action.

    The fourth step of the lesson is the reading of the text. Again, the method of reading is determined by the practice. The whole text is read orally in guided reading, while the text is read silently, paragraph by paragraph, in transitional guided reading. This step of the lesson is where the eyes and mind hit the print. It is also the prime assessment opportunity in the lesson.

    The fifth step of the lesson is the return to the text. Whatever the readers do while reading the text determines what the teacher returns to. This is where the explicit skill, vocabulary, and strategy teaching takes place. This is also where the teacher guides the children in metacognition so their problem-solving actions become clear to them.

    The last step of the lesson is the response. Responses—which may be oral, written, or visual (including three-dimensional)—drive children back into the text and provide different catalysts for them to express their understanding and the connections they make with the text. (Chapters 7, 8, and 9 describe the teaching sequences for different instructional practices.)

Q.   What do you say to children when you sit down with them over a book? How do you get them to read it and understand it?

A.   The most powerful tool a teacher has is his or her voice. What we say to children directs their thinking. Time spent in a lesson is short and precious, so we must make every second count. In guided reading, we guide children's thinking, and reading comes from thinking.

Teacher talk falls into three categories. One category is *coaching statements*. These are positive statements that tell children what they know or remind them what they know about. These statements initiate thinking. They are a positive start that points the children's thinking in the right direction. Another category of teacher talk is *questions*. These are interrogatives that stir the thinking. These questions get the children to think in terms of possible routes of problem solving or solutions to problems. We need to be careful to avoid the "have you ever" and "how many of you" questions. We use these as a means of including and building relevance, but too often they redirect the thinking away from the author's intent. The third category of teacher talk is *prompts*. These are statements that give direction; they tell the children what to do. These three types of teacher talk ignite the thought processes as children strategize, and they keep the children's thinking going in the right direction. Guiding children's thinking is like herding cats: the coaching statements, questions, and prompts are the prods we use to keep their thoughts moving along a somewhat straight, not-too-wide path.

We question, coach, and prompt children for two purposes: inquiry, which happens before and during the reading and takes the children into and through the text, and metacognition, which happens during and after the reading and takes the children through and out from the text. Knowing what to say at each point in the lesson requires a high level of expertise, because teacher talk does not come in a script. What we say is literally determined by what the children say and do. Excellent teacher talk makes you teach on the edge of your seat. (Chapter 4 discusses the types of teacher talk and when and how to use each one.)

NOW WHAT?

I guess the only thing left to do now is to read the book. I hope you enjoy the ride and maybe learn a thing or two. I work full-time at a university now, training those who want to teach reading and writing and those who strive to learn even more. My role there is to help teacher candidates think about what they would do. In addition, I continue to work as a staff developer and still do not want to change what you do; instead, I want you to think about what you currently do. It is still a wonderful time to be a teacher working with teachers and those who aspire to the role. So much to learn and so little time . . . let's get started.

Part I

Foundations

Chapter One

How Learning Happens

CHAPTER OVERVIEW

The good news is that we are wired for learning. Our species has continued this long that we must be designed for survival. So how do we make the most of this penchant for learning? Learning theory after learning theory after learning theory has been offered throughout the ages. This chapter investigates one such theory.

In walking, attaching one step to another gets you somewhere. In learning, attaching one bit of knowledge to another gets you somewhere. When we attach new information to existing information, we construct understanding. Connections between smidgens of knowledge are like scaffolds—you know, those lengths of wood or metal that attach to each other to form a sturdy foundation upon which to work. Generally, the teacher aligns the planks or bars and works to ensure that they are connected in the students' minds. Over time, the scaffolds eventually become bridges from one bit of knowledge to the next.

What are these bits of understanding? All lessons that result in some form of learning contain five parts:

- concepts

- skills

- vocabulary

- strategies

- behaviors

These five elements form current and next learning. In this chapter, we look closely at the first three items on the list. Strategies and behaviors will be discussed in detail in Chapter 3.

LEARNING AS A SCAFFOLDING PROCESS

The bits of understanding that one has control over—that can be used, in other words—form the foundation of current knowledge. Our job as teachers is to determine the specifics of which concepts, skills, vocabulary, and strategies each child has control over and can use. Like all humans, children know a lot more than they use, so we need to assess how much the children use of what they know. We also need to measure the degree to which they use it and the level of alacrity with which they use it.

We have to do these things so that we can know what the child needs *next*. The operative word here is *next*. We cannot provide what children *need* because they need everything. The best we can hope for is to provide what they need *next*. Once we know what they have in place, we can determine which concept, skill, vocabulary, or strategy they need next. The new learning is attached to existing learning. Figure 1.1 illustrates this process.

Figure 1.1   Learning as a Scaffolding Process

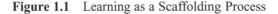
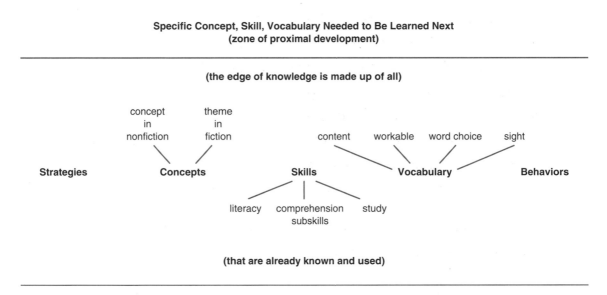

CONCEPTS

Concepts are what the children are going to learn about from a particular text. The concept is generally the theme in fiction and the specific content in nonfiction. The teacher needs to be clear about what the children are expected to learn from an instructional text, and should tell them what the book is about. This single simple bit of knowledge arms them with a shelf of understanding prior to encountering the book. Knowing what the book is about sets up an array of expectations and corridors of access, and prepares the reader to interact with the book more deeply and more immediately. Consider the following scenario:

> *A teacher walks around the room showing everyone the book* Charlotte's Web *by E. B. White. It is the classic version with the traditional cover. The title is written in spiderweb-like print, and the dominant characters in the story are shown in the cover illustration, with the girl and the pig particularly prominent. The teacher tells the children that this will be their next read-aloud and that she is going to read a chapter every day after lunch. She tells them they will enjoy this story because it is one of her favorites. She reads them the title, the author's name, and the illustrator's name. Then she asks the timeless, universal question: "What do you think this story is about?"*

Why do we ask children this question? What are we really asking for? When did this ritual become a good idea? When questioned, teachers generally say something about "having children use prior knowledge" or "having children make predictions." But are the children really drawing on prior knowledge? Really predicting? You be the judge.

Suppose one child raises his hand and asks, "Is it about a girl named Charlotte?" Is he drawing on prior knowledge? Is he predicting? He uses the two slivers of information he has: the title of the book, which often provides a hint and in this case contains a girl's name, and the illustration, which contains a dominant figure who happens to be a girl. He puts those two bits of information together and, using his prior knowledge that Charlotte is a girl's name, decides that the book must be about a girl. But is *Charlotte's Web* about a girl? No, as the teacher explains to this little guy, a girl is in the story, but the story is not about that girl. So, was the child predicting? Nope. He was just guessing. He had only those two slivers of information, which were not enough to make an accurate prediction. He *was* using prior knowledge, but not in the way the teacher had hoped.

Suppose another child raises his hand and says, "Is it about a pig named Charlotte?" This child uses three bits of information: the title, the illustration, and his classmate's error. This fellow discounted the name as strictly a girl's name and went with the possibility of it being the name of the second dominant figure, the pig. Clever, yes, but still not right. (Not that being right is important.) These children are not even in the ballpark. The teacher knows it is time to move on when the third child raises her hand and asks, "Is it about Charlotte's Web site?"

So, what is the difference between making predictions and guessing? Guessing happens when we have minimal bits of information. Predictions require personal input. Predictions are *schema* events. Ah, schema—a scary graduate school word! *Merriam-Webster's* defines it as "a mental codification of experience that includes a particular organized way of perceiving cognitively and responding to a complex situation or set of stimuli." I prefer my own definition: the sheet of fabric that billows behind us as we walk through life. Everything we encounter either sticks to or slides off the sheet; the stickier our sheet, the more that adheres—events, impressions, everything. The more that sticks, the stickier our sheet becomes. What lingers on our schema sheet serves as a sieve, shaping all thoughts and ideas as they pass through.

So predictions, as opposed to guesses, are based on more than fragments of data. But back to the Charlotte. . . . What is *Charlotte's Web* about? No, it is not about a spider either! The girl, the pig, and the spider are all characters, and like most stories, the book is not about characters. Stories are generally about something bigger than the characters—an idea, a theme. This concept is what the characters live in, work toward, demonstrate, personify. *Charlotte's Web* is about friendship. There, *that's* the concept: friendship, and all that is friendship.

Think about how the children might have responded if the teacher had told them, "This is a story about friendship." Their brains would have done a file search for "friendship" and come back with all sorts of friendship-related ideas and experiences. They would have been so much better prepared to make predictions. Their thinking would have been so much more centered and driven.

Now, back to our scenario. Let's suppose the teacher has finally let on that the book is about friendship. The conventional question at this point would be something like, "Have you ever had a friend?" Now why in the world would anyone ask such a thing? Of course the children have had a friend. Instead of asking a "have you ever" question, we need to go directly to the point and tell the children, "You know about friendship." This focuses their thinking and immediately engages them, rather than causing them to ponder a yes-or-no question. At this point, when the children are wrapped up in the idea, the teacher needs to say, "Tell me what you know about friendship." Here the children begin to share relevant experiences, define friendship, describe friends, and pretty much build a profile of what it all means. Now they are ready to make predictions—predictions that are on target and meaningful. *This* is powerful thinking. *This* builds on the existing scaffolding—it sets the stage for learning.

SKILLS

Skills are behaviors we learn that we can use for a greater good. They are useful only within a context: learning skills in isolation makes them useful only in isolation. Skills are nuts and bolts that enable us to hold together words, sentences, paragraphs, stories, ideas, and understandings. Having control of skills enables us to process more information, and to process it more accurately and quickly. We will discuss three types of skills here: literacy skills, study skills, and comprehending skills.

Literacy Skills

Literacy skills fall into several subsets—reading skills, writing skills, listening skills, and speaking skills—but the skills in the various subsets are reciprocal. In other words, reading skills are used in writing, and speaking skills are used in listening. All of these skills are taught and learned throughout all the grades, but in this chapter we focus on reading skills. These are identified teaching points and features to note within a context when we are conducting reading and writing lessons. Some reading literacy skills are listed in Box 1.1.

Box 1.1   Examples of Literacy Skills

Abbreviations	Digraphs	Possessives
Alphabetical order	Diphthongs	Prefixes
Apostrophes	Grammar	Punctuation
Blends	Letter names	Root words
Capitalization	Morphemes	Suffixes
Compound words	Phonemes	Syllabication
Contractions	Plurals	Verb tenses

Literacy skills are explicit and rather minute. They include the names of individual letters, the sounds we give those letters and letter combinations (also known as phonics), and the ways we arrange those combinations of letters to form words (also known as spelling). They include the mechanics of how to wrangle words into phrases and sentences (also known as grammar), and how to delineate those sentences as organized masses (also known as punctuation).

Literacy skills include puzzles about words that look alike but sound different and mean different things, as well as words that look different but sound alike. They allow us to break a word when we run out of room in a line, and to work through a word using chunks of letters. They make it possible to change the meaning of a word by adding letters to the front or the end of it, and to recognize the heart of a word that has additional bits stuck to the front and the end.

While literacy skills are tiny, isolated bits of information, the role they play in language is huge. They permit us to designate some words as more important than others. They allow us to talk about many of something, rather than just one. Literacy skills include the bits of information that enable us to refer to events that happened in the past as well as those that will happen at some point in the future. They allow us to own things.

"Do we still teach skills?" folks ask. We never stopped teaching skills. Today, however, we recognize the importance of helping children *use* the skills they are learning.

Study Skills

Study skills enable children to interact with texts in ways that strengthen understanding and provide vehicles for expressing that understanding. Study skills help children to do five things:

- locate information
- record that information
- retrieve that information
- manipulate (move) that information
- use that information

The nature of the information involved depends to a large extent on the subject matter as well as the motivation for learning. Box 1.2 presents a partial list of the kinds of information that study skills enable children to gather and use when reading or learning to read.

Box 1.2   Types of Information Targeted by Study Skills

Character traits and indicators	Key words
Definitions	Plot points
Details	Word explanations
Evidence of setting	

Children who learn how to *locate* information in a book are prepared to ferret out the specifics of the author's intent. These children have greater control over working through the unknown. A primary source for locating information in a book is the table of contents. In addition, elements such as the index, the glossary, headings, footnotes, sidebars, callouts, and captions are all sources for locating information in nonfiction texts.

Once students have located information, they need to be able to *record* or mark it in some way. Some useful tools for this are highlighter tape, erasable highlighter pens, sticky notes, and temporary glue sticks with adding machine tape. These tools enable students to temporarily mark the information at its source on the page.

When the book is closed, the information disappears into it. At some point, however, that information will be needed again. The third function of study skills is to enable children to *retrieve* information already found and marked. An effective tool to use for this is edge tabs, or sticky notes that hang out from the edge of the book. Every time a child marks a word or phrase in the text, he or she copies that same word or phrase, and the page number, onto a sticky note and places it in the margin. The result is what kids call a "hairy book." The edge tabs help the children to quickly retrieve the bits of information.

After the information has been placed on the edge tabs, the tabs can be peeled from the book pages and moved to another place. This process enables the reader to *manipulate* the information. Manipulating the information means changing its place and purpose. For example, the edge tabs can be organized into a list, can be used to build an outline, or can form the basis for note cards. Such flexibility with information is empowering. The reader now owns that information and is able to put it to use.

The whole reason for teaching children study skills is so they will be able to *use* the information they have found. For example, the outline and note cards mentioned above can be used to write a report. Nonfiction key word edge tabs can be alphabetized and evolve into a glossary or index. Key words can also be used to write captions, footnotes, or sidebars. For fiction, key word edge tabs for character traits can be used to design a character map. Storyboards and time lines can be diagrammed using key word edge tabs for dimensions of setting and plot points.

Comprehending Skills

Comprehending what has been read is the reason we teach reading. Our work and that of the children is not about the reading, and never has been. The work is about the *thinking*. Nothing matters if the children do not know what it is they have read.

Comprehending is conjuring an image from the author's words and the reader's experiences. It is maintaining that image, shifting it as the words and experiences indicate. Comprehending remains intact as long as the reader sustains the image and realizes when the image breaks.

Comprehending requires taking mental action with the text. Box 1.3 shows a list of some of the forms of comprehending. (Notice that each word is a verb; comprehending skills involve the reader in interacting with the text or taking action with the author's meaning.)

Box 1.3 Examples of Comprehending Skills

Knowledge—gathering information; on the page; see it and do it (on the page)

Count/Quantify	List	Practice	Sequence
Define	Match	Recall	State
Describe	Measure	Recite	Tell
Draw/Illustrate	Memorize	Recognize	Trace
Find/Locate	Name	Recognize patterns	Write
Identify	Observe	Record	
Label	Outline	Remember	

Comprehension—confirming and connecting (in the head)

Change	Explain	Interpret	Recognize errors
Clarify	Extend	Model	Relate
Confirm	Generalize	Paraphrase	Re-state
Connect	Infer	Plan	Summarize
Distinguish	Inquire	Predict	Verify
Expand	Instruct	Prove	

Application—making use of knowledge (with the head and hands)

Apply	Dramatize	Hypothesize	Relate
Change	Draw/Sketch/Paint	Make	Show
Choose	Experiment	Model	Simulate
Collect	Explain	Modify	Solve
Demonstrate	Express	Predict	Visualize
Design	Formulate	Prepare	
Diagram	Gather alternatives	Produce	
Discover	Generate	Quantify	
Discuss	Graph	Question	

Analysis—taking apart (with the head and hands)

Analyze errors	Determine	Investigate	Select
Categorize	Differentiate	Organize	Separate
Classify	Dissect	Point out	Sort
Compare	Distinguish	Problem solve	Subdivide
Contrast	Examine	Qualify	Survey
Decide alternatives	Graph	Research	Take apart
Deconstruct	Infer	Revise	

Synthesis—reducing, combining (with the head and hands)

Add to	Design	Invent	Rationalize
Combine	Develop	Originate	Summarize
Conclude	Formulate	Organize	Synthesize
Construct	Generalize	Plan	
Deduct	Hypothesize	Produce	

Evaluation—judging, value laden (with the heart)

Appraise	Contest	Establish a position	Reason
Apprise	Criticize	Evaluate	Recommend
Argue a position	Critique	Judge	Relate
Assess	Defend	Qualify	Weigh
Consider	Develop an opinion	Rationalize	

Guided reading lessons for children learning to read focus on strategy building, which enables children to make the meaning or read the words. Strategies form the foundation for comprehending. They help children to self-monitor—to recognize when the meaning breaks down or the text isn't making sense.

Once children can read and have begun to master the strategies they need to self-monitor, the focus of reading instruction shifts from the making of meaning to comprehending the layers of meaning within the text. Transitional guided reading, the instructional practice that follows guided reading, focuses on tying the reader's mind to the text. In transitional guided reading lessons, the teacher focuses the children's thinking on one or two specific elements in each paragraph, setting them up to read for a particular purpose in that paragraph. The children read silently and then debrief the focal point with the teacher, who next sets them up to read and think through the following paragraph. In this way, teacher and children work through the text, with the teacher laying the framework for comprehension *before* reading, rather than waiting to check comprehension afterward.

Vocabulary

Words have always been the stuff of reading instruction. While there are many types of vocabulary, we will discuss four here: sight words, workable words, content words, and word choice.

Sight Words

Sight words are toeholds in a mountain of unknown text—those words that are automatically readable. They are the words the reader recognizes. Sight words include environmental words as well as words that have personal meaning to the reader. Environmental words might be words on fast-food containers; words on bags from shopping trips; the names on cereal, cookie, and cracker boxes; the names of favorite shops and food places; or other automatically recognized words. Word walls, word banks, and full-sentence labels around the room help increase the number of sight words over which a child has control.

Workable Words

Workable words are those words a child can work through. There are many ways to work through a word. While working through words involves reliance on literacy skills, sounding the words out is only one way to figure out the words. Only about 60 percent of the words can be decoded in the English we speak. (That might sound like a lot, but 60 percent is rarely enough to make and maintain meaning.) In guided reading, emergent readers learn a repertoire of strategies that enable them to use all the sources of information to work through words. Early readers use those strategies in guided reading, and practice makes strategy use more and more automatic.

Content Words

Content words are those words directly related to a concept. It is generally easy to locate content vocabulary in nonfiction text as often the words are indicated in bold or italic print, or the book may have an index or a glossary. In fiction, the content words deal with the concept or theme of the story. Content vocabulary in fiction can be found in words used to indicate characters, setting, and plot. Words or phrases, even scenarios, that indicate a concept such as courage or adventure are examples of content vocabulary in fiction text.

Word Choice

Word choice refers to the conscious decisions a writer makes to use one word over another. Beautiful language, such as a well-placed adjective or colorful metaphor, represents word choice, as does powerful language such as strong verbs. While beauty is in the eye of the beholder, the teacher can shape what children identify as beautiful language and powerful verbs. The more we point out examples while reading, the more likely the children are to take note of what they see as beautiful or powerful language. Over time, children begin to assimilate what they are learning, and we begin to see evidence of word choice in their own speaking and writing.

Chapter Two

The Continuum of Development

CHAPTER OVERVIEW

As teachers, we base all our decisions concerning instruction on our students' behaviors. Through their behaviors, children demonstrate what they can use from all that they know. Their behaviors help us to determine their stage of development, and therefore which instructional practices are most appropriate.

Like other types of learning and behavioral development, the acquisition of literacy occurs along a continuum of increasing flexibility and application. In this chapter, we look at the literacy continuum, which consists of six developmental stages:

- preemergent
- emergent
- early
- newly fluent
- truly fluent
- proficient

After an overview of the continuum, we examine each stage of literacy development. The discussion includes details regarding typical behaviors and appropriate instructional practices at each level. Also included is information on the meaning of the widely used term "fluency," and on the behaviors that mark fluency in reading.

OVERVIEW OF THE LITERACY CONTINUUM

Figure 2.1 depicts the literacy continuum and the sequence of reading instructional practices. Note that the density of the arrow at the top reflects the nuances of learning acquisition rate. The younger the children, the faster and the more they learn (see Figure 2.1).

Figure 2.1   The Continuum of Literacy Development

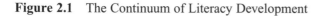

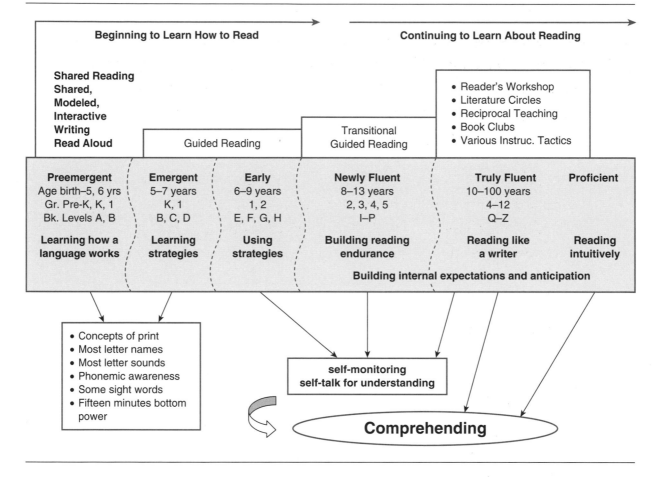

THE PREEMERGENT STAGE

Preemergent is the stage of development from birth to about age three or four, sometimes five. These children are learning how the language works. They are learning to speak and understand the language, how it sounds to the ear and feels in the mouth. Preemergent readers are getting ready to learn how to read, and they need to learn the six literacy behaviors that prepare them for the rigors of guided reading:

- concepts of print
- names of most of the lowercase letters
- most of the sounds we give letters and some letter combinations
- some sense of phonemic awareness
- some sight words, including environmental words
- fifteen minutes of "bottom power"

These basic literacy behaviors continue to develop in emergent readers, those at the next stage of development. In prekindergarten, kindergarten, and Grade 1, these basic units of learning take place during shared reading, shared writing, modeled writing, interactive writing, language experience, independent journal writing, and independent reading, as well as during small-group skill work with letters and little books. Preemergent and emergent readers need to see themselves as readers and writers. These practices make up a great deal of the day at the lower primary level but also continue through the grades. Only the purpose changes. (For more on the six literacy behaviors and some of these instructional practices, see Chapter 7.)

If they are to become literate, children need to use the tools of literacy. As they do so, pre-emergent behaviors manifest themselves and are refined. For example, a preemergent writer will frequently make lines or use symbols to represent written words. A preemergent reader will talk through or tell a story while turning the pages of a familiar book. The children's interactions with books or paper and pencil indicate how well the basic literacy behaviors are developing. That evidence forms the first informal assessments.

THE EMERGENT STAGE

Emergent children, typically ages four to about six or seven, are learning what the language can do. They learn that what they say can be written down and that what is written down can be read. Emergent learners are ready to learn strategies that enable them to read with less and less support from the teacher. The purpose of guided reading is to teach children those strategies, and it is with children at the emergent stage that guided reading begins.

Emergent reading behaviors include beginning to recognize sight words other than environmental words. Children at the emergent stage begin to use the pictures in books as clues to what the text might say. Soon these children begin to cross-check from the picture to the text, comparing the sounds in the words for what they see in the picture to the letters they see in the words on the page. Gradually they begin to recognize when something doesn't sound right, when the grammar or semantics don't make sense. Emergent readers read one or two lines of text on a page. Patterned text, obvious rhyme, oral language structure, simple sentences, and ample-size print with white space are supports for the beginning reader.

Emergent writers are moving away from scribbling or random letter and symbol use. The structure of their writing begins to take on cultural forms, with perhaps spaces between words and the use of periods at the end of statements. Emergent writers begin to write the letters they hear, frequently most of the consonants in a word—for example, "wnt" for "went" and "slbrprtte" for "celebrate." Occasionally, consonants with similar sounds are substituted for one another, as in "wyast" for "watched" and "dsne" for "Disney." Slowly, vowels begin to appear as placeholders. That is, the vowel may not be correct, but a vowel sits in the place where one should be—for example, "thu fod wus gdu" for "the food was good." Children at this stage sometimes write two words as one, just as they are combined when heard—for example, "wda" for "one day," "hip a" for "help pa," and "ranovr" for "ran over." They begin to copy words from the environment, including the items from the classroom word wall and words they find in books, and on posters and charts around the room. Emergent children are quickly learning and using many tiny literacy bits. The emergent stage of development is a period of natural acceleration in learning.

THE EARLY STAGE

Early readers, typically ages six to eight or perhaps even nine—Grades 1 through 3—make up the third stage of development. These are children who are applying what they have already learned. They are still learning how to read but are getting stronger and more immediate in their use of what they are learning. All children at the first three stages of development are learning the concepts, skills, vocabulary, and strategies that make them readers.

Guided reading instruction continues with children at this stage. Because early readers are more automatic in their use of reading strategies and are more consistent self-monitors, these children read more lines of text with less need for the kinds of supports necessary for emergent readers. Early writers' writing looks more standard. It also shows evidence of the specific phonics and language arts skills and vocabulary being taught in the classroom. For example, an early writer might write "folload" for "followed," indicating a knowledge of multiple formations of the long /o/ sound. The early reader and the early writer are using what they know and are getting stronger and more immediate.

Early readers continue to learn strategies for making meaning from print. More importantly, they begin to use those strategies to self-monitor. (Self-monitoring is discussed in Chapter 3.)

WHAT IS FLUENCY?

The words "fluent" and "fluency" are two of the many "beach ball" words in our profession—words teachers bounce around all the time. ("Yes, I teach for fluency"; "They need to build their fluency"; "Well, he's so fluent!") What does fluency really mean, though?

In terms of reading, fluency can mean various things. At its most basic, it is simply a continuously existing state of being somewhere along the literacy continuum. Consider an eighteen-month-old child looking out the window of a car. Up ahead, he spots a red and white sign. He knows that shape, he knows that sign—yes, yes, it's a Dairy Queen! Obviously, this child possesses a degree of fluency. But he is less fluent than a child who bursts into tears at the end of *Stone Fox*.

More technically, the term "fluent" is applied to a particular portion of the literacy continuum. It is the level that follows the emergent and early stages where children are just beginning to learn to read. Because fluency in reading represents a rather broad stage during which a significant shift in instructional strategies is appropriate, the literacy continuum divides fluency into two stages: newly fluent and truly fluent.

Fluency in reading is marked by certain observable behaviors. These include:

- comprehension
- accuracy
- smoothness
- reading increasingly challenging text

Comprehension

The first and most important behavior that marks fluency is comprehension. It doesn't matter how well a child reads if he or she doesn't understand what has been read. Comprehension is indicated by a reader's capacity to interact with the text via a variety of comprehension subskills. (See Chapter 1 for further details.)

Accuracy

Accuracy contributes to comprehension but is not necessarily meaningful in itself. Actually, many children read with a high degree of accuracy but don't have a clue about what they've just read. (These accurate but mindless readers are called "false positives.") True accuracy comes from self-correcting, which occurs when a child makes an error, realizes it, and takes steps to correct it, all without the teacher's assistance. This, in turn, requires that the child be able to self-monitor, or realize that what he or she has just read doesn't make sense. Self-monitoring is one of the first indicators of comprehending and is a primary target of reading instruction.

Smoothness

A third fluent behavior is the ability to read smoothly, not just quickly. This is not the same as "reading with expression." Too often, false positive children read with expression that results from an appreciation and use of the rhythm of the language and a control of punctuation. Expression is frequently misinterpreted as an indicator of comprehension, but false positive readers are simply skilled performers.

While expression in itself is meaningless, children do need to learn to read like they talk. Some newly fluent children read word by word, almost poking at each word. Having them sweep a finger along the text may help to develop smoothness.

Increasing Challenge

The ability to read increasingly challenging text is what differentiates newly fluent readers from truly fluent readers. Simply put, the newly fluent children are getting stronger as readers. They are putting what they know to use, learning to self-monitor on the fly, and learning how to comprehend what they are reading. But to do all of this, they tend to read a lot of similar materials, such as series with recurring characters and related plot lines. As they move from the newly fluent stage to the fully fluent stage, children are able to move beyond such familiar and comfortable material and tackle various genres and new authors.

THE NEWLY FLUENT STAGE

Children at the fourth stage of development are called newly fluent. They are typically seven-through ten- or eleven-year-olds, second through fourth or fifth graders. These are children who can make the meaning or read the words. They have automatic control of strategies, and they self-monitor on the fly. They do read, and they are getting stronger as readers. As mentioned earlier, they seem to enjoy reading series of books that have recurring characters and are of the same genre. Newly fluent readers take to these books because of the support they offer—there is limited risk in reading another mystery by the same author that contains the same characters getting into and out of the same scrapes. To use a workout metaphor, these are children who are increasing the reps before adding more weight.

Newly fluent children are often called "good readers." ("Oh, he's such a good reader! He reads so beautifully.") They may indeed sound good, but how much of what they are reading is really getting behind the eyes? Newly fluent readers are at a critical stage of development because they are at risk for two detrimental outcomes: aliteracy and false positiveness.

Aliteracy occurs when an individual knows how to read but chooses not to. We see more and more aliterate children every day. Children today have so many options available to them. Why should they read? The newly fluent stage is where children are at greatest risk for aliteracy.

False positive children can read beautifully but don't have a clue about what they have just read. They often cannot answer even the most basic questions regarding content. We are also seeing more and more false positive readers. These children need to learn how to think as they read.

Transitional guided reading is the instructional practice for newly fluent children. The focus of transitional guided reading is comprehension. This is where teachers tie the children's minds to the text. (Transitional guided reading is discussed in detail in Chapter 9.)

THE TRULY FLUENT STAGE

The fifth stage of development is called truly fluent. When children have reached this level, not only can they read, they can understand what they are reading. Unfortunately, many teachers feel that these children no longer need instruction. Nothing could be farther from the truth! These children still need help, to prepare them to think and understand more independently. Instructional practices such as reader's workshops, literature circles, reciprocal teaching, and book clubs shift increasing levels of various types of responsibility for independent thinking and understanding onto the reader. (These practices are discussed in Chapter 9.)

THE PROFICIENT STAGE

The last stage of development along the literacy continuum is proficiency. Most teachers are proficient readers. At this point, instruction is moot, since proficient readers read not because they want to read, they read because they have to read. Proficient readers are fully addicted to print; they have a literate monkey on their backs.

Rarely are proficient readers without something to read. Consider this scenario: you are preparing to attend a workshop or meeting and, without even realizing it, you slip a little something to read into your bag, just in case the session doesn't go the way you thought it might. Sound familiar? Another example: you are in an elevator and what do you do? Read every word of the "certificate of inspection." We've all done it. . . .

Proficiency is our goal for children. We want to turn them into wanton consumers of text. We want children to read and talk about what they've read. We want kids to wait and pine for the next book by whomever. How do we get them to this point? Consistent, continuous, excellent teaching makes it happen. Nothing else.

Chapter Three

The Reading Process

CHAPTER OVERVIEW

Reading is making meaning from the printed word. To make meaning, the reader uses a number of sources of information. These sources, also known as cues, include:

- pragmatic sources

- graphophonics

- syntax

- semantics

- schemas

- sight words

- human sources

In order to process information sources to make meaning, the reader uses strategies. Learning to use strategies is therefore essential to learning to read. Actually, learning to read has two parts: learning to use strategies and learning to self-monitor. Emergent readers learn strategies. Early readers use those strategies to self-monitor. Each guided reading lesson facilitates the learning and use of strategies.

In this chapter, we examine some of the more important information sources in the context of guided reading instruction. We then look at strategies and at literate behaviors, which teachers can observe to gain insight into children's thought processes as they read. Finally, we look at self-monitoring, the first level of comprehending.

INFORMATION SOURCES

Pragmatic

A task is less burdensome, perhaps even more enjoyable, when we know why we have to do something. Rationale means a lot at times. One of those times is in guided reading.

The teacher needs to tell the students the reason for reading the book. This is done in the first step of the teaching sequence, while setting the scene. In addition to giving the children the concept of the book, or telling the children what the book is about, the teacher should also explain why this is the book for today. Among the reasons might be that the book is fun, or is by an author they have already encountered, or deals with something they already know about. The reason can be as simple as, "I picked this one for you. I thought you might like it."

Graphophonics

English is a code-based system. The code is made of symbols (letters) and values (sounds). Letters themselves do not have sounds. (Actually, they have many, which can be troublesome.) The reader or speaker gives the letters sounds. The sound we give a letter depends on its placement in the word. About 60 percent of the words can be sounded out in the English that we speak. (That may sound like a lot, but it is not enough to achieve a high enough degree of accuracy to make and maintain meaning.)

Try your hand at "decoding" the following. Pay attention to what you are doing as you make the meaning.

I 7tX£8'yE COtIET OCVXE TO **tiiE** (AX7 o4) 'r'ile YvtirES Imam o4) Apeptixa.

So what does it say? Did you figure it out? If not, try it out on someone else and see how that person does. If you're still in the dark, here's a hint: it's the first line of a promise American citizens make. Now do you know it? Sure: "I pledge allegiance to the flag of the United States of America." Of course!

For those of you who did figure it out, what did you do? Probably you scanned the whole thing, looking for something to grab on to. For some of you that worked hard on the problem, you might have been caught by the uppercase letters, lingering on the final words until your mind told you they were something like "United States of America." Although some of the symbols were unfamiliar, the graphophonics were a very powerful cue. If this information source worked for you, your brain probably then did a mental file search of familiar phrases containing those words. Your eyes ran back to the front of the sentence and began to search again for other symbol combinations that looked like something.

Or maybe you scanned the line and found something that looked familiar—perhaps it was the words that kind of looked like "to the." Then you scanned again and found another "the." You scanned again and your brain used those two bits as placeholders while you continued to scan and rescan, sifting all the other bits until something else fell into place—perhaps the word "I." Like rock climbers, we grab on to anything that sticks out for us. (Actually, everything that you did, each mental process, was a strategy. Even those who didn't get it until you read the translation used a strategy known as appealing. But we'll get to that later.)

In order to benefit from guided reading lessons, emergent children need to know the names of most—though not all—of the lowercase letters and the sounds we give to most—though not all—of the letters and letter combinations. Literacy-building programs in most kindergarten and first-grade classrooms provide a lot of letter and sound work opportunities for children throughout the day and week. Most emergent children will know most, if not all, of the lowercase letters by the time they begin their first guided reading lesson. In too many classrooms, however, formal reading instruction is delayed until children have control of every upper- and lowercase letter, even those that are used less often, such as *z* and *q*. Programs that introduce one letter a week can actually delay children's broader interactions with print. Many teachers love letter-of-the-week programs since this approach organizes instruction so nicely. What's good for the teachers, though, is not always best for the children.

Syntax

Every spoken and written language has certain principles of word order. Put another way, if something is to make sense, certain kinds of words can sit next to only certain other kinds of words. This word chain is syntax, or grammar.

Syntax is developmental in nature. For example, a young child might come bursting in the back door huffing and puffing and say, "I runned and runned!" This child is overgeneralizing a rule that has made its way into his field of knowledge: to form the past tense of a verb, you add "-ed." Pretty good for a little one. At some point, the child will learn that "run" is an irregular verb.

As teachers and parents, we monitor the language our children use and model for them the forms of language inherent to our culture. We also directly correct or influence the children's speech. Consider this exchange between a kindergarten teacher and a five-year-old one Monday morning:

Child: Teacher, teacher!

Teacher: What? What?

Child: This weekend, me and Jimmy . . .

Teacher: Jimmy and I.

Child: No. Me and Jimmy, we . . .

Teacher: Jimmy and I.

Child: No. Teacher, you weren't there.

Children readily learn syntax from guidance, modeling, and direct intervention. As their language skills develop, their grammar becomes more broad based.

Semantics

Many words have multiple meanings. The term "semantics" refers to the commonly held meanings of words. The meaning a word has is determined by its place in the sentence and the context in which the sentence sits. Consider the example, "Blue Gill is a sad cowpoke," appearing in a story about cowboys. The cowboy context and the capitalized first letters establish the meaning of "Blue Gill" as the name of a cowboy, a proper noun. Now consider another example, "I caught a blue gill in my net," appearing in a story about fishing. The fishing context gives evidence that the meaning of "blue gill," as used here, is a type of fish. It could also be said that "blue" is an adjective modifying "gill," a common noun. Both explanations are correct.

Schemas

A schema is the sieve through which all experience passes. Our schemas shape what we know and how we know it. The schematic source of information includes those words that have personal meaning. For example, consider the words we use within the family to describe body parts and body functions. These words have meaning within the walls of our house or within the arms of our loved ones. But people outside those walls or arms may not understand the words.

Many times, semantic meaning is compromised by what our schema does to the word. That is, word meanings can be influenced by what is heard and what is understood. A fourth-grade teacher offered this example. She was setting the scene for a new story and said to the children in the group, "One of the characters in this story is a bandit. You know what a bandit is?" All of the children nodded and the teacher asked one of them to explain what a bandit is. "It's like on a ship," the student said. "What?" asked the teacher. "Yeah, like on a ship. When the ship begins to sink, you abandon it." This shows a potential lack of understanding.

Another example comes from a transitional guided reading lesson I did with a group of second-grade boys. The children were reading "Little Deer," a story that begins with a deer trying to cross a river. The boys encountered a word that conjured up a different mental image than the one the author intended. I had just asked the boys to read a page silently, telling them that here they would find the first of several solutions the deer would try. They dropped their eyes and began to read, but soon all the heads popped up with odd, confused looks. The first sentence on that page says, "Little Deer walked to the bank." What caused their confusion? The author meant riverbank; the boys were thinking financial institution!

Figures of speech can be impacted by schemas. I was doing a transitional guided reading lesson with a group of fifth graders using a story in their reading anthology. The lesson had been going along really well, with all the children participating and everyone responding as directed. Near the middle of the lesson, I set the children up to look for a character indicator in a paragraph. The sentence I had in mind said something like, "Sarah is constantly underfoot." I told the students they would find another detail about the main character. I asked them to read the paragraph silently and put up a thumb as a signal that they were ready to discuss what they found out. I watched as every student read the entire paragraph. No thumbs. I asked, "Well, what did you find out about Sarah?" No one said anything. After much coaching, questioning, and prompting, I finally told them that what they were looking for was in the last sentence. Still nothing. What was going on? Who were these kids and where were the ones who had been here a few minutes ago? Finally I said, "You, read that last sentence out loud." The student did: "Sarah was constantly underfoot." I said, "There, right there, what did the author just say about Sarah?" No one said a thing. In desperation I said, "Someone say something! There is no way you can be wrong." Finally one girl said, "You know, I was wondering about that." "What, what were you wondering?" I asked. She said, "I never imagined Sarah to be that small."

How could those children not know the meaning of that figure of speech? They simply had no experience with it. It was not a part of their schema, and schema shapes all meaning. Schematically, they interpreted the words "underfoot" literally, because they knew no other meaning. I was surprised that these students didn't know the correct meaning and so was their teacher, who was observing. But the moral of the story is to assume nothing and give children an opportunity to prove you wrong.

Sight Words

Our lives may be littered with them, but sight words are often overlooked in the reading realm. Frequently, teachers incorrectly label children as "nonreaders" when actually these children have wide, deep pools of sight words. Sight words are words that are automatically recognized and have meaning. They come in several forms:

- **"Orthographic" words:** These are words that are of high interest and are important to the reader personally. For whatever reason, children seek out and learn to read many words. For example, little boys in kindergarten who cannot make out color words can often read the names of dinosaurs or snakes. Consider the first grader who was able to read and write the name of a popular headache medicine. When asked how she knew that word, she explained that her mom had headaches and this little girl was often sent to the medicine cabinet to fetch the pills. If a word is important to them, the children will find a way to get to it.
- **Environmental words:** These are words that are important in daily living for each child. For example, many young children are extremely literate while cruising the cereal aisle of

the grocery store. Fast-food restaurants and takeout containers are the reading stuff of many young family members. Names of favorite shopping places are quickly recognized and understood.

Kindergarten teachers who want their youngsters to see themselves as readers can gather up empty fast-food containers as well as food packages that are typically found in homes with young children—cereal boxes, milk containers, catsup bottles, and so on. Shopping bags from local discount department stores are also good. These items can be placed in baskets or boxes on the first day of school and set out on the carpet for children to "go see how many things you can already read." Granted, many of the children will know the name from the container rather than actually reading the word. The point is that these children need to see themselves as readers and believe they can read. The focus on the specific words that identify the item will come later.

- **Lexical words:** These are instantly recognized words. Frequently they are nonphonetic words that cannot be decoded, such as *have*, *want*, *was*, and *gone*. They are also high-utility words such as *is*, *the*, and *and*. Traditionally, such sight words have been taught in isolation. Flash cards abound in primary classrooms. Sometimes the number of sight words a child has control of is even recorded for all to see. However, a concern about this method of sight word instruction is that all too often the child is not able to recognize the word in other places. What is the big deal if a child can read a bunch of words in isolation, anyway? The only other time in his or her life where that might happen is if the child serves as the pronouncer at a spelling bee. The goal is to get kids to automatically read and understand words within a context.

Labeling the room is nearly ritual room preparation in primary grades. The teacher writes words on cards to identify items around the classroom and then sticks those cards next to the items they identify. Sometimes this is done before the children even arrive at school, and never actually discussed with the children. Labeling the classroom is a practice that should continue, but if teachers want it to contribute to the establishment of a literate environment, they need to engage students in the process.

One way to ensure that children encounter words in context is to label the room in full sentences, with the children participating. On the first day or so of school, take a field trip around the room with children, locating and discussing each of the areas and features. For example, stopping by the classroom library, you might tell the children something like, "This is our library. All of these books . . ." and then go on to tell them the rules for using the books. The next stop might be the pencil sharpener. Begin with, "This is our pencil sharpener. We can sharpen . . ." and go on to discuss the whys and wherefores of pencil sharpening. The third stop might involve the wastebasket and the finer details of trash management. Each stop on the trip begins with the same line, "This is our . . ." This stem sets the scene for a shared writing or language experience activity on the following day.

For shared or modeled writing the next day, pin a sentence strip to the easel. With marker in hand, lead a discussion of some of the items and places visited on the classroom field trip. Have a child go to each item or site as it is mentioned. Say, for example, "Yes, this is our wastebasket. Let's make a label for it so visitors will know what it is. Let's write, 'This is our wastebasket' on this sentence strip and then we'll tape it to the wastebasket. Let's count the words in our label." Together with the children, count the number of words. Each day, make a new label using the same stem, "This is our," until the places and items in the classroom are all labeled. As you write each word, work through the letters and sounds together with the children. The children will learn the sights and sounds of each of the words that make up the stem of the sentence. Someone will probably notice that "is" has the same letters that "this" has, for example.

The classroom word wall is another resource for building up a sight word vocabulary. Word banks, lists of important words, and spelling lists are all valuable tools for sight words, but the true power of sight words is realized in a greater context.

Human

For a child learning to read, the human source of information is the teacher and the other children in the group. The teacher's role is obvious as he or she coaches, questions, prompts, or even tells the word to the readers as they process the text. The other children in the group help each other as they process along.

STRATEGIES

The sources of information described above are pools of language data the reader dips into. Each of us and each of the children carry these language pools around. The degree to which we automatically use them determines the level of fluency we have.

The integration of these sources of information takes place through the use of strategies. (Ah, strategies, another inflated word in our profession. Everyone has strategies: assessment strategies, organization and management strategies, playground strategies, you gotta have 'em. So of course we need some strategies here!) Within the context of reading, strategies are the in-the-head decisions a reader makes to figure out what the text says.

Functions of Strategies

Strategies are the root of literacy learning. They serve as the mental manual for processing text. Strategies are what a reader does in his or her head when meeting an unknown word. They serve a number of functions. For example, they enable a reader to:

- draw on stored information
- problem solve words
- detect and correct errors
- build toward and maintain fluency

Sample Strategies

During guided reading lessons, students learn a variety of strategies. Each strategy provides a different type of problem-solving action. Guided reading helps children to gain control of strategies, and to learn to use more than one at a time as they read. The following are samples of strategies a reader might use when stalling on a word.

- **Cross-checking:** The reader uses more than one source of information to confirm or discount a prediction in order to construct meaning.
- **Sampling or searching:** The reader scans the various sources of information, such as looking at the picture, looking for sight words or familiar words, or looking for a repeating pattern.
- **Predicting:** The reader uses what is known about the story to determine what the text might say or mean. The reader can also use the illustrations to anticipate the meaning.
- **Reading into a word:** The reader continues looking at all the letters and hears all the sounds that make up the word, rather than stopping at the first letter and guessing.
- **Skipping a word and reading on:** The reader skips a word in order to use the rest of the sentence to increase the context. The reader then returns to the unknown word and uses the extended context to figure it out.
- **Rereading:** The reader returns to the beginning of the sentence and rereads the sentence to get a running start using the sense of the sentence up to that point.

- **Sounding it out:** The reader hisses and spits the sounds given to each letter that makes up the word. This is the universal and frequent first choice of beginning readers.
- **Leaning on Margaret:** The reader leans into the child next to him or her and listens to what that child says.
- **Appealing:** The child asks what the word is, generally without hesitation.

Each of these strategies is useful by itself. It is the teacher's responsibility to get the children to use multiple strategies. This is done through the teacher talk, discussed in Chapter 4.

LITERATE BEHAVIORS

We cannot see what a reader is thinking because we cannot know what is inside another person's head (which is actually a good thing!). Therefore, if we want to know what is going on in there, we must rely upon the observable evidence the reader shows. Likewise, we cannot assess what a child knows; we can only assess what that child does with what he or she knows. During a guided reading lesson, the teacher observes literate behaviors demonstrated by the children as they process the print during the oral read. The following are a few of the behaviors that children demonstrate while reading. You will notice that some of these behaviors are also strategies.

- **Stopping or stalling:** The reader encounters a word that is unfamiliar or unknown. Stopping or stalling is the trigger behavior that indicates the child is self-monitoring.

- **Substituting:** The reader uses a word that makes semantic and syntactic sense but may not be a graphophonic match with the text—for example, "What is the trouble?" for the correct, "What is the problem?" "Trouble" for "problem" is not a bad substitution because the words match syntactically, as they are both nouns and they are semantically similar. They do not look alike, however, so they are not visually (graphophonically) similar.

- **Inserting:** The reader adds words to the text that the author did not write. These types of embellishments may result from a language pattern error, a schematic override, or an overactive imagination. For example, instead of the correct text, "Under my bed I have socks," a child might read, "Underneath my bed I have socks." This is a language pattern error. The child's oral language is "underneath." (The teacher may or may not choose to address the error. In this case, I would not, since the usage is colloquial and does not change the meaning.) An example of a schematic error is seen in the example of a child reading, "I smell orange juice" for the actual text, "I smell oranges." This kind of error may be difficult to analyze. In this case, we really don't know whether it is the result of schema or attention to the illustration, which shows a glass of orange juice surrounded by orange slices. An example of the third type of insertion behavior, overactive imagination, might be when a child says, "The cat leaps over the water to the other side" for "The cat can jump." Maybe the child is not letting his or her ability stand in the way of a slacker author. Or perhaps the child is using the picture, which does show a cat apparently leaping over a body of water, presumably landing on the other side. Again, it may be difficult to analyze the source of the behavior.

- **Omitting:** The reader skips an occasional word while reading. The number and type of words that are skipped and the frequency of this behavior may indicate that the text is too hard, or that the child has shallow spots in his strategy repertoire.

- **Sounding out:** A strategy as well as a behavior. The reader attributes a sound to each letter and letter combination that makes up the word.

- **Self-correcting:** The reader uses multiple sources of information, checking one against another and ultimately correcting a miscall. Self-corrections are occasions for engaging in metacognition with a child to determine how he or she figured out the correct word. They are also causes for celebration.

- **Pointing:** The reader uses a finger to indicate what words he or she is seeing with the eyes and reading with the mouth. Emergent readers are encouraged to point. Early readers begin to sweep their finger under a line of text as their rate of reading increases. Pointing behaviors begin to fade over time, but return when troublesome text is encountered. Newly fluent readers continue to sweep, and may need to use a narrow line marker as they encounter increased text density.

- **Returning:** A strategy as well as a behavior. The reader returns to the beginning of a sentence to reread a phrase or the whole sentence in order to confirm or discount a prediction. Used too often, this becomes choppy reading.

- **Choppy reading:** The reader slowly works through the words in a sentence, and rereads but does not confirm, over and over again. Choppy reading indicates that the text is too hard for the reader.

- **Appealing:** The reader stalls on a word and looks to the teacher or another child for help. The frequency of this behavior may indicate the number and types of strategies a child has or how secure the child is in using those strategies.

SELF-MONITORING

Once an arsenal of strategies and behaviors is learned and used, the next step is to use them to recognize when the meaning breaks down. This is called self-monitoring, and it is the first level of comprehending. Self-monitoring involves that silent, almost subliminal, conversation we have with ourselves as we read. It is what we say to ourselves as we process print.

It is essential that children keep a running self-dialogue going on in their heads as they are reading. This running commentary keeps a reader focused on the author's message and prevents the mind from straying from the print to ideas and thoughts that are not related to the text. The self-talk serves as a voiceover for the streaming video of images the brain conjures from the author's words. Like a voiceover, the self-talk explains, enriches, extends, and comments on what is seen. This conversation with the self—self-monitoring—keeps the brain's thinking in line with the author's words. In the early reader, reading behaviors are the problem-solving strategies of stopping when what has been read does not make sense; slowing down or stopping to work on words; going back to reread a phrase, sentence, or entire part to check whether it sounds right; and making personal comments about what has just been read.

Reading instruction is about thinking. Self-monitoring is thinking. Guided reading instruction is about building a storehouse of immediately accessible strategies in the beginning reader.

Part II

Techniques

Chapter Four

Teacher Talk

CHAPTER OVERVIEW

Have you ever wondered why this instructional technique is called *guided* reading? What are we really guiding? Sure, we guide the children as they read. But what specifically are we guiding?

In its purest form, each guided reading lesson is an opportunity to guide the students' *thinking.* As teachers, we guide the students to think in certain ways in order to solve problems or revisit their problem solving. We do so using our most powerful tool: our voice. In other words, what we say to the children orients their thinking. This "teacher talk" focuses their thinking and causes them to make mental decisions, thereby streamlining the problem solving before, during, and after the reading. Teacher talk is the root of strategy building.

Teacher talk falls into three categories:

- coaching statements
- prompts
- questions

Each type triggers specific mental actions that activate, sustain, and reflect upon thinking.

Teacher talk serves to take children into, through, and out from concepts, skills, vocabulary, and strategies. The specific type of teacher talk we use is determined by what the children do at the point where coaching, prompting, and questioning are needed. Teacher talk influences two main types of thought processes: inquiry and metacognition. Teacher talk that triggers inquiry processes takes readers into the sources of information before and during the reading. Teacher talk that triggers metacognitive processes takes readers out from the sources of information during and after the reading.

In this chapter, we first look at inquiry and metacognition in the context of guided reading, then focus separately on each of the three types of teacher talk. The elements of teacher talk are summarized in table form at the end of the chapter.

INQUIRY AND METACOGNITION

As discussed in Chapter 3, strategies are the specific mental problem-solving decisions a reader makes to figure out individual words and to work out what a combination of words (a sentence) means. Strategies involve selecting one or more sources of information and mentally manipulating those bits to determine what the print says. We coach, question, and prompt children to make inquiries of the various sources of information before and during the reading. Doing so drives their thinking into the various aspects of problem solving, which is the very essence of strategy building.

Once children use strategies, we need to ensure that they realize that they are indeed taking specific actions to figure out the words. Have you ever tried to get the computer to do something new? You pull down menus you did not even know you had. You begin to randomly hit buttons followed by "backspace, backspace." But you get nothing that looks like what you want. More indiscriminate hitting of buttons, then all of a sudden, after minutes of aimless button pushing, it happens! Yes! Finally! At such times, our first thought is, "What happened? What did I just do?" We want to know what we did so we can do it again later. So we metacognize. In other words, we rethink our steps, examining exactly what we did and in what order.

In the same way, we coach, question, and prompt the children to revisit and reflect upon their problem solving during and after the reading. This type of metacognitive teacher talk enables the children to rethink exactly what they did to figure out the words. We encourage the children to discuss their in-the-head actions. When they articulate their problem-solving decisions, their thinking becomes obvious to them and the others in the group, and they are more likely to use those strategies again.

COACHING STATEMENTS

The old adage that we get more with honey than with vinegar holds true for literacy development. Coaching statements are positive statements. They remind children what they already know. Starting with a coaching statement initiates a positive first encounter with the text, and as humans, we tend to respond with positive strength to positive stimuli.

Coaching statements for inquiry position children's thinking before and during the reading. They direct the children into the various sources of information and remind the children what they already know and know how to do. The following are examples of inquiry coaching statements.

- You know about . . .
- You are good at . . .
- You know what that word/sound/picture is.
- You know how that should sound.
- You know what to do.
- You've seen that word before.
- You can figure out that word.

Such potent comments enable children to focus their thinking and cut through potential uncertainty. Being told that we know or can do something is powerful. Humans tend to believe what they are told at the point of telling. Why not take the opportunity to trigger a positive first thought by coaching the readers?

Anything the teacher says initiates a mental file search. A coaching statement such as "You know what colors cats can be" focuses the children's thinking on cats and their colors. Each child's brain does a file search, sifting for cat experiences, then narrows that thinking to the colors of cats. Good coaching statements are specific and influential. In contrast, consider the typical question, "Have you ever seen a cat?" Of course students have seen a cat! Why even ask such a silly question? Yet many of us do ask children these kinds of inane, low-level questions in the name of building relevance. Such questions risk distancing a student who may not have had the experience, or who thinks we mean a live and literal experience.

We also coach during and after the reading. Metacognitive coaching tells the children what it was they did to solve the word. This is valuable if the children are unaware of what they did. Emergent children, especially, may lack the awareness to realize the importance of their mental actions. So it falls to the teacher to point out those actions. The following are examples of metacognitive coaching statements.

- You caught that mistake.
- I saw you working.
- You figured out that word.
- You looked at the picture.
- You went back and tried it again.
- You knew that didn't sound right.
- I saw you look at the picture.
- You used the picture and the word.
- You read into that word.
- You are good at using the letters and sounds.

These are things we say to children to reinforce their thinking. They are positive reminders of work done well, rather than reminders of what the children do not yet know or cannot yet do. Success begets success.

PROMPTS

Sometimes a gentle, well-placed nudge is just enough to get the job done. Prompts are gentle nudges the teacher gives to direct the children's thinking. Prompts give direction. They tell children what to do. Generally, we initiate an encounter with a coaching statement to set up the children's thinking, and then we prompt to keep the thinking headed in the direction we want. The following are examples of inquiry prompts:

- Look at the picture.
- Look at the word.
- Show me where that is.
- Put your finger on it.
- Look at the letters.
- Get your mouth ready.
- Read into that word.
- Say it out loud.
- Read it again.
- Read on.
- Skip it.

What we prompt the children to do is determined by what they have just done. Prompts direct the children's actions so their thinking is more purposeful. These kinds of statements enable the children to operate with a certain amount of success. Over time, children begin to assimilate these kinds of thoughts, and they begin to do them automatically.

When children initiate a strategy, we want them to know what they did. Metacognitive prompts direct children's thinking back to the explicit strategy and urge them to verbalize their problem solving. Metacognitive prompts direct the children to recall and state their mental actions. The following are samples of metacognitive prompts.

- Tell me how you figured that out.
- Show me where you found that.
- Show me where you looked.
- Read it like we talk.
- Explain how you know that.
- Tell why that's the word.

QUESTIONS

Teachers ask a lot of questions. But not all questions are created equal. Good questions stir and direct thinking, as do the other forms of teacher talk. And, like other teacher talk, good questions foist the responsibility for thinking onto the children.

Inquiry questions trigger the neural connections that link one source of thinking with another. They funnel the children's thinking to decipher or strategize upon specific elements of the text. Inquiry questions tend to be open in nature, which allows for multiple answers. The child's response to an inquiry question indicates where he or she was looking and what he or she was thinking. A well-timed, well-placed question can tie up loose threads and nudge a student to solve the puzzle. The following are samples of inquiry questions.

- What can you do?
- Where will you look?
- What would make sense there?
- How does it start?
- How does it sound?
- Will that match?
- What do you see?
- What do you think he/she/it would say/do/feel/want/think/need?

These questions situate the children's thinking so that they can couple several sources of information and improve the efficiency of their problem solving.

Metacognitive questions serve the same purpose as the other types of metacognitive teacher talk. These questions direct the children's thinking back onto their problem solving. The following are examples of metacognitive questions.

- How did you do that?
- What helped you?
- Where did you look?
- What did you hear?
- Why did you stop?
- Is that it?
- Does that word work?
- How do you know?
- Is that what the author wrote?

Like questions for inquiry, these questions are relatively open ended and allow for multiple responses. The purpose, again, is to enable the children to realize the focus and power of their thinking—in other words, to make their thinking obvious to them.

MORE MATURE READERS

The examples in this chapter apply directly to emergent and early children working at the word level in guided reading. However, coaching, questioning, and prompting are needed with newly fluent and truly fluent children as well. For children in transitional guided reading, reader's workshop, and literature circles, teacher talk concerns the development and expression of ideas. We coach, question, and prompt newly fluent and truly fluent readers to discuss the nuances of the theme or concept within a story, and facets of the writer's craft. With these more mature readers, the talk about the text deals with layers of meaning—comprehending the message beyond the page.

SUMMARY

Table 4.1 summarizes teacher talk and gives sample statements and questions. One interesting, and perhaps unexpected, benefit from the consistent use of these forms of teacher talk is the children's assimilation of it. We know what we are doing makes a difference when we see our own behavior and hear our own voices in the children. A while back, a teacher shared that she had overheard one first grader coach another who had stalled on a word: "Go ahead, honey, you know that word. Look at the picture. You know what that is." Children learn what we teach them. Let's teach them what counts.

Table 4.1   Summary of Teacher Talk

	Inquiry	Metacognition
	Talk that takes readers into the sources of information before and during the reading	*Text that takes readers out from the sources of information during and after the reading*
Coaching statements	• You can figure that out. • You know that word. • You know what to do. • You've done this before. • You know what sound that has.	• You caught that mistake—good work. • I saw you working. • You did a good job. • You looked at the picture—good work. • You knew that didn't sound right.
Prompts	• Look at the word. • Look at the picture. • Look at the letters. • Read it again. • Say it. • Point to it. • Skip it. • Read into it. • Read on. • Say it out loud.	• Tell me what you did. • Show me where you looked. • Read it like we talk. • Explain how you know that. • Tell why that's the word.
Questions	• What can you do? • How does it start? • Will that match? • Where will you look? • How does it sound? • What do you see? • What do you think he/she/it would say/do/feel/want/think/ need?	• How did you do that? • Where did you look? • Why did you stop? • Does that word work? • Is that what the author wrote? • What helped you? • What did you hear? • Is that it? • How do you know?

Chapter Five

Grouping Schemes

CHAPTER OVERVIEW

"Instruction" is a term widely used in our profession. We talk about the "instructional day" and "whole-group instruction" (the latter is actually an oxymoron) to describe what we do with children. However, instruction does not occur every time a teacher stands up before students. Instruction is a specific type of interaction. It is finite and focused. Instruction is the laser surgery of teaching and results in changed behavior. After instruction, the learner now knows something—in other words, has attached something new to what is already known, and is ready to put that new knowledge to use.

Reading instruction results in changed literate behavior. For this change in the learner, instruction requires an intimate dynamic. The degree of intimacy is determined by the size and makeup of the group.

In this chapter, we will first look briefly at instruction and guided practice—which take place in groups—before examining the different types of grouping schemes in terms of the dynamic, purpose, makeup, shelf life, and management of each group. We will then focus on the finer details of scheduling groups for reading instruction. Finally, we will take a look at the special cases of triads, pairs, and "onesies"—how they work and when they are appropriate.

INSTRUCTION AND PRACTICE

Instruction is one part of the learning process. It is preceded by awareness—the "heads up" for what's to come—which readies learners for the specific content of the instruction. Instruction requires a degree of intimacy that smaller numbers provide. Following instruction, guided practice ensures that what has now been learned is applied as intended. Guided practice involves sitting with a small group and nudging their application of the material. The teacher shows the students, and then hands the material over and watches them do it while coaching and prompting and questioning. Sounds like guided reading!

Guided practice is something we too often skip. We teach, assume the teaching has paid off in learning, and then go straight to independent practice—the next step in the learning process.

Independent practice requires some kind of feedback so the learner has a clue as to how well he or she is doing, or how closely he or she is meeting the expectation or standard. Too often, the only feedback children get is a negative response to a job not done well enough. Independent practice with feedback means the learners need to know right away what they did well and how they can improve the bits that need it. Work done as seatwork or as homework, such as responses to reading, are examples of independent practice with feedback.

More often than not, learning requires a waltz between guided practice and independent practice with feedback, back and forth. Ultimately, the knowledge is assimilated into the schema and is automatically accessible and utilized. This is independence.

THE HETEROGENEOUS CLASSROOM

Most American classrooms are heterogeneously organized. "Heterogeneous" means made up of many kinds, like a bowl of fruit or a can of mixed nuts. Heterogeneous classrooms are generally made up of some children who are at grade level, some who are above grade level, and some who are below grade level. Figure 5.1 illustrates the makeup of a heterogeneous classroom.

Figure 5.1   A heterogeneous classroom is made up of children who represent a range of development. The faces symbolize that range.

The teacher's job is to do whatever is needed to ensure that each child learns, and is able to use what is learned. To do this, the children and the teacher interact in various ways within the classroom. These encounters involve whole groups, large groups, and various types of small groups, as well as sessions with triads, pairs, and individuals. Each type of group encounter provides a different type of learning or application opportunity, because each offers a different dynamic. The group dynamic is the degree of intimacy the children have with the teacher. Children need to have a variety of interactions in order to ensure that what is taught is learned and what is learned is used.

WHOLE GROUPS AND LARGE GROUPS

American elementary class sizes typically range on either side of twenty or twenty-five children. Everything mentioned here, in the context of whole-group and large-group encounters, is relative based on the number of children who make up a classroom. Whole-group encounters involve all the children and the teacher attending to a single task. Large groups involve half the children and the teacher attending to a single task. The other children not involved in the large-group event, the "loose" ones, are engaged with other activities.

For a teacher, interacting with ten to thirty children can be a challenge, generated by the sheer number of brains, eyes, and mouths involved. The dynamic, or degree of intimacy, a teacher has with a whole or large group is broad and shallow. The best the teacher can hope for is to spray the learners with information.

Indeed, whole-group encounters are like watering the garden. The children are the flowers and the teacher is the gardener. The gardener has a good hose (curriculum) with a quality nozzle (materials) and excellent water pressure (expertise). The gardener adjusts the nozzle to just the right setting, turns on the water good and strong, and begins to spray those flowers. The gardener is patient and thorough as the flowers in the garden are sprayed. Some of them, the tall ones near the top, get soaked. "Enough already!" they plead, "I've had enough! I've already been watered plenty." Some flowers are nourished. "Ah, yes, yes, that is good!" they say, "a little more, a little more." And some of those flowers, the short ones underneath, say, "What? Did you feel something? Huh?"

This is not to say that we should not do whole- or large-group encounters. We should and we must and we do. In fact, a large portion of the day is spent in whole-group interactions. We need to realize, however, that the broad, shallow dynamics of whole- and large-group events provide for only a superficial treatment of the concepts, skills, and vocabulary being addressed. But "superficial" is not used here in a derogatory sense. It simply means that the broad dynamic prevents the teacher from going too deep or too high in his or her teaching. By their very nature, whole- and large-group events target the middle, and in so doing lose the ends.

Whole and large groups do provide a climate that is appropriate for awareness, initiation, demonstration, and modeling. Examples of whole- and large-group encounters that illustrate this include reading aloud, reading along, shared reading, shared writing, modeled writing, language experience, and whole-group direct teaching. None of these is instruction, but each is an integral step that sets the stage for further learning. Whole- and large-group encounters often precede later small-group encounters. Children spend the bulk of the day in a combination of whole-group, small-group, and individual pursuits. What is addressed in whole- or large-group sessions must be addressed again in a small group at some point.

SMALL GROUPS

Ability Groups

Many of my age-mates—those looking at retiring in a few years—remember when we "used to do small groups." "Aren't we going back to what we used to do?" they ask. Well, no. Someone once said, "We must not forget the past lest we are doomed to repeat it," or something like that. So, no, we are not going back to anything. We can't go back because we now know so much more about literacy development and brain research. Furthermore, what we used to do was ability grouping, and ability groups do not have a place in classrooms today.

I wager that each of us remembers exactly what reading group we were in at school. Top-group folks are usually the first to share what group they were in. I was never a top-group kid. I was, and remain, happily planted smack dab in the middle. Which is my point. Generally speaking, once a middle-group, top-group, or bottom-group kid, always a middle-group, top-group, or bottom-group kid. The die is cast and there we pretty much remain. Ability groups are forever. They are organized based on the gross manner in which learners access, process, and apply information. Isn't it interesting that when it came to literacy, schoolchildren seemed to fall into three piles, sort of like laundry? So how do we group children for instruction if not by ability?

Homogeneous Groups

More precise teaching allows for greater learning. The type and number of students who interact with a teacher in a teaching–learning event impact the precision of the teaching and thus the amount of learning. Working with the right type of students in a group allows a rhythm of teaching and learning to take place. Working with the right number of students in a group allows an optimal degree of intimacy. Ideal situations allow for a rhythm of teaching and learning to develop over time. Enough rhythm may lead to a momentum of learning. Over time, that momentum may result in a natural acceleration of learning.

Children participate in a number of small-group formations during the school day. Some small groups are for practice and some are instructional. Practice groups may be cooperative, social, interest oriented, project oriented, and so on. But our purpose here is to discuss instructional groups. Instructional groups are homogeneous.

To increase the precision of the teaching so that more learning takes place, the teacher should work with a few students at a time. Instructional groups for reading are small groups made up of four to six emergent, early, or newly fluent children, or four to seven or eight truly fluent children. They are composed of children who know and use the same concepts, skills, and vocabulary right now, and who access, process, and apply information in the same way and at the same pace right now. Teaching a homogeneous group is like teaching a four-, five-, or six-headed child. It's teaching four, five, or six kids as though they were one. The makeup of the group sets the standard for performance for each member of that group.

Figure 5.2 illustrates how the children in a heterogeneous classroom are organized into homogeneous groups. The number and range of children in the illustration warrant the formation of five homogeneous groups.

Homogeneous groups are formed on the basis of data the teacher has obtained. Initially, data are gathered from the formal and informal assessments the teacher conducts in the first weeks of school. A variety of assessments combine to form a profile of a learner's current literacy status. The specific types of assessments used are determined by the student's stage of literacy development and what types of information the teacher wants to find out. Concepts of print, sight words, letters and letter combinations, the sounds associated with letters and letter combinations, and strategy use are all useful bits of information that help in forming homogeneous groups of

Figure 5.2   Homogeneous groups are made up of those children who know, use, and need the same concepts, skills, and vocabulary. These children access, process, and apply information in the same way and at the same pace.

emergent and early readers. Assessments for emergent and early learners include reading records, letter and sound assessments, and writing samples. Assessments for newly fluent children include reading records, writing samples, and comprehension checks.

Flexible Grouping

As you probably noticed when you read the description of homogeneous groups for reading instruction, the emphasis was on "right now." Instruction happens in the present. Because of this, homogeneous groups are relatively short term in nature. Since the teacher is working with so few children at a time, he or she is in an excellent position to see learning, or the lack of it, taking place. Being able to observe the nuances of learning take place in the children who make up the group enables the teacher to notice the subtle changes that indicate differences in learning among those children. These differences, subtle though they may be, may become more obvious. When this happens, it generally indicates to the teacher that a shift in the degree of homogeneity within the group has taken place. What is a teacher to do when a group becomes less homogeneous?

Over the course of several lessons, as the teacher begins to know the learners and expect certain behaviors from them, he or she may begin to notice slight changes in an individual. A child may be the first with ideas, be the first to respond, or be slick as silk in his or her reading. The teacher may think, "Who lit a fire under *you*?" This child has taken off in his or her learning. This child is now the alpha dog in the group. Will this child now serve as the leader? Is that a bad thing?

Well, the good news is that this child has taken off in his or her learning. The bad news is that this child has taken off in his or her learning. Why is this a bad thing? Because now the dynamic of the learning has changed. "Homogeneous" means "the same," and this group is no longer homogeneous. This group now has a top dog. A leader.

Humans are the top-functioning animals on the planet, but we are still animals. In the animal world, a leader will always emerge, as has happened in this group. The leader realizes on some deep, primal level that he or she is the leader, and as such, this child instinctively operates to guide the others. So, this alpha child assumes leadership behaviors and continues to lead and become even stronger, sensing a responsibility for the others in a "Follow me, boys!" sort of way. The other children in the group, being the animals they are, realize on that same, primal level that So-and-So is the leader and that they are subordinate to him or her. As subordinates, the other children defer to the leader's abilities and may actually slack off, allowing the leader to do their job in a kind of "Lead on, we're right behind you, big boy!" way.

Because we are human too, we tend to teach to the one with strength—which means we tend to teach to the strongest kid in the group. It is wonderful to work with kids who are getting it! We end the lesson thinking, "Boy, that was good. What a great lesson; I am such a great teacher!" And then we whine when we realize the others didn't get it.

Keep in mind that the opposite scenario might take place. All is going along fine with a group, and at some point the teacher notices a child falling behind. The dynamic has shifted again. The child who has fallen behind may pull a great deal of the teacher's energy and attention from the others. So what is the teacher to do? How can he or she reestablish the homogeneity? The only thing to do is move those individuals who are no longer homogeneous. But move them where? Into another instructional group, of course.

What about stigma? Don't the kids know which is the "smart group" and which is the "dumb group"? Come on, of course they know which group is which. Then what about their self-esteem? Won't they feel bad if they are in one group and not another? At some point, we have to stop lying to the kids. Someone has to say, "I love you—I am the teacher who is going to keep you reading and keep you getting better as a reader. I will never lie to you; I will only do what you need to make you a stronger reader and thinker. You are lucky to have me; now sit up and get ready to learn." The intensity, intimacy, pace, and rigor of reading instruction through guided and transitional guided reading lessons are such that success is encountered. Part of what makes the lessons intense, intimate, and rigorous is the teacher's expertise in pulling together the right group of kids, giving them the right book for that day, and doing the best lesson possible. And then doing that day after day after day, until the kids achieve a rhythm that becomes momentum, which then becomes acceleration.

Ideally, a teacher organizes the children into four instructional groups, seeing three groups each day. (Depending on the number of children in the room, a teacher may instead end up with three or five groups.) Occasionally, however, the children don't all fit into four neat groups. Sometimes, one or two children are not homogeneous with the established groups. So do we have a group of one or two? No, as we will see later, one or two children working with a teacher will not provide a dynamic appropriate for instruction. Then what do we do with the one or two who stick out?

Deployment

It is the teacher's responsibility to find just the right group for each child. Sometimes the right instructional group for a particular child is in another room. Deployment is sending a child across the hall or next door to a room where there is a group of other children who are learning just like him or her right now. Deployment, or platooning, takes place only during the lesson time. The child is out of his or her room only during the fifteen to thirty or so minutes of the lesson. The deployed child does not pack up his or her things and move to the other room.

On occasion, deployment involves children from different grades, which can be a sticky situation. What happens when a second grader, two third graders, and a fourth grader are homogeneous? Whenever possible, we try to send the children up the grades. So, the second and third graders go into a fourth-grade classroom for the lesson. Fine for the second and third graders, but what do we say to the fourth grader sitting there with these little kids? When in doubt, try the truth. I tell the fourth grader that the other children are with him or her right now and he or she has been selected as the mentor for these children. This is the truth. The fourth grader, while homogeneous with the younger children in his or her literacy learning, will offer maturity to the others, however slight.

Various discussion points concerning deployment need to be worked out. For example, which teacher gets the mixed-grade group, how can we coordinate all the schedules so that deployment can work, who gives the literacy grade, what do we tell the parents, and who conducts the parent conference? These issues can all be worked out. Teachers across the nation have generated a litany of reasons why deployment can't work in their schools. The bottom line is that it is the teacher's responsibility to do what is needed to ensure that each child's literate behavior increases over time. These questions call for professional negotiating. The solutions exist—our job is to find them.

SCHEDULING

As mentioned earlier, a teacher typically organizes the children into four groups (although class size may warrant three or five groups), seeing three groups each day. Generally, instructional lessons last from fifteen to thirty minutes. Guided reading lessons for emergent and early readers last fifteen to thirty minutes. Transitional guided reading lessons for newly fluent children last about thirty minutes. Reading instruction lessons for truly fluent readers may last thirty to forty minutes. This is not a long time. Instruction is precise and focused, which allows for a fairly quick pace.

The frequency of lessons is determined by the stage of development of a group. With the limited time teachers have to do all that is needed, we are forced to resort to a kind of literacy triage:

• **Emergent learners** have farther to go and thus need to meet with the teacher more often. Usually, the more emergent learner has less bottom power and therefore benefits from shorter, more frequent lessons. Beginning learners, whether literacy learners or language learners (ELL), need constancy to ensure their learning—they need to meet with the teacher more frequently. The most emergent children may meet with the teacher four or even five times each week for perhaps twelve or fifteen to twenty minutes each lesson.

• **Early readers** are those children who have learned the strategies that make them readers. These children are using the strategies in guided reading. Early readers need to meet with the teacher at least three times each week in lessons of twenty or twenty-five minutes.

• **Newly fluent readers** are those children who can read and are now focusing on comprehending. These children are getting strong as readers in transitional guided reading lessons. Since comprehending what is read is the focus for these children, newly fluent readers should meet with the teacher three times each week in lessons of twenty-five or thirty minutes.

• **Truly fluent readers** are those children who can read and think on the fly, but they still need instruction. Truly fluent children are reading away from the teacher and therefore need to meet with the teacher less often—perhaps twice a week in lessons of thirty or thirty-five minutes.

Table 5.1 illustrates one rotation of groups in a five-day week. It shows which group is seen when and the length of each lesson. This schedule is only one suggestion. Other schedules abound and provide for other school day requirements such as special events, lunch, and so on.

Table 5.1   Weekly Small-Group Instruction Schedule

Monday	Tuesday	Wednesday	Thursday	Friday
Group D 15 mins	Group C 20 mins	Group B 30 mins	Group C 20 mins	Group D 15 mins
Check-up—who needs me, who has what done and goes where, who does what?				
Group C 20 mins	Group D 15 mins	Group A 30 mins	Group D 15 mins	Group C 20 mins
Check-up—who needs me, who has what done and goes where, who does what?				
Group A 30 mins	Group B 30 mins	Group D 15 mins	Group B 30 mins	Group A 30 mins

- **Group D** is least independent group and needs small-group instruction most often. Group D meets with the teacher five days a week for small-group reading instruction and other times each day for additional reading and skill work.
- **Group C** meets with the teacher four days a week for small-group reading instruction and other times each day for additional reading and skill work.
- **Groups A and B** are more independent and need less—three days—small-group instruction with the teacher. Groups A and B engage in more independent reading work.
- **"Check-up"** refers to the few minutes at the end of a small-group lesson and before the next one begins where the teacher checks up with who needs help, who has what work finished, and who needs a talking-to. It is also the time for guiding the children into what they are to do next. These breaks between lessons ensure that the students get their teacher fix and are not working independently for too long. After time, the routine of lesson, check-up, and sift establishes a comfortable rhythm that provides an important element of the social environment within the classroom.

At first glance, it appears that the students are on their own for fairly long periods. But note that the "loose" ones—those children who are not in the current instructional group but are working independently at their seats or at centers—are without immediate teacher supervision for only the fifteen to thirty minutes of each lesson. At the end of a lesson, the teacher dismisses that instructional group back to their seats and then "checks up" with the rest of the class. This is the few minutes—three to five at the most—the teacher takes to check in with the kids, answer questions, put out fires, settle disputes, grant permission for pencil sharpening, and so on. The children come to know that the longest they will have to wait for the teacher's attention is until the lesson is over. True, this can be a lifetime to little ones, but they grow into the understanding.

The daily schedule in Table 5.2 illustrates what the others might be doing independently while the teacher works with one group. Independent work takes many forms that generally fall into two categories: seatwork and centers, or a combination of the two. Essential to the success of enabling children to work independently is training the children how to live together with the teacher in the classroom. Training takes time, sometimes the first thirty days of school. Many teachers are uneasy about not taking groups for the first month or so. However, groups cannot be formed until the children are assessed, which takes time. Those first weeks of school are for finding out what the students know and can do. At the same time, the students learn the rules of the roost, which establishes the pecking order for the rest of the year. The more successful the children are at working independently, the more successful the small-group lessons will be. As stated earlier, intimacy is a critical factor in ensuring that learning occurs. Nothing breaks intimacy quicker than being interrupted. The time spent at the beginning of the school year building independence pays off later on with increased and perhaps accelerated learning.

Table 5.2   Daily Small-Group Instruction Schedule

			Check-Up		Check-Up		Check-Up		
	10–15 minutes	15 minutes	15 minutes	15 minutes	15 minutes	15 minutes	15 minutes	15 minutes	15 minutes
Group D	Whole-group events: Read-aloud	With teacher in small group	Reading response work	Journals	Listening center	Computer center	Word work center	With teacher in small group	Whole-group events: Read-aloud
Group C	Shared reading/writing Mini-lessons and transitions to independent work	Journals	Listening center	With teacher in small group		Reading response work	Word work center	Computer center	Shared reading/writing Mini-lessons and transitions to other content areas
Groups A/B		Journals	Computer center	Listening center	Word work center	With teacher in small group		Reading response work	

TRIADS, PAIRS, AND ONESIES

If four, five, or six homogeneous children form a dynamic that is appropriate for instruction, is having fewer children better? Not necessarily. As stated earlier, instruction results in changed literate behavior. Having fewer than four children constricts the dynamic and chokes the instruction. Therefore, groups of fewer than four children should be formed only for special purposes.

The dynamic in a very small group does provide an interaction that is appropriate for intervention, remediation, or reteaching. Intervention takes place before the learning "goes bad." Remediation happens after the learning has gone bad, and may require student unlearning. Reteaching is teaching something again in the same way, generally with the same materials. Each of these types of encounters is different and necessary.

Groups of three, two, and one-on-one are very short term and are often skill groups. The close intimacy allows the teacher to work even more precisely with the students. The tight proximity ensures that the teacher is able to provide the exact concept, skill, or vocabulary those few children need next.

Working with fewer children at a time enables the teacher to make eye contact with each of them, speak with each of them, and focus the teaching on only what each of them needs right now. Working with fewer at a time increases the intimacy and therefore the affect. A lot of learning deals with heart as much as, if not more than, mind.

Chapter Six

Analyzing Texts

CHAPTER OVERVIEW

Guided reading and other small-group reading instructional practices are success-based encounters. One way to ensure success is to give children text that is not too hard, not too easy, but just right. But how do we measure "just right"? What does that even mean? For a long time, the terms "instructional," "independent," and "frustration" were used to describe how right a book was for a particular group. Today we know more about how learning happens and how instructional texts are constructed.

In this chapter, we first look at general considerations for choosing instructional texts for reading. We then look at specific considerations for choosing books for readers at each stage of literacy development, using five criteria:

- concepts and content
- language, vocabulary, and word study
- illustrations
- sentences and sentence structure
- text layout

Concepts and content are the ideas within the book—what the book is about or what the children will learn about. Language, vocabulary, and word study deal with the actual words that make up the text. Illustrations are the images that accompany the print. In wordless books and simple label books, the illustrations are the text. Sentences and sentence structure are concerned with the type, number, and length of sentences. Text layout pertains to the placement of illustration and text on the page. Illustration style, size of print, and the amount of white space between letters, words, and lines are additional text layout considerations.

The analysis of texts by literacy level using these five criteria is summarized in table form at the end of the chapter.

GENERAL CONSIDERATIONS

Guided reading lessons are conducted with a book selected by the teacher. Both fiction and nonfiction books may be used in guided reading lessons. Generally, guided reading lessons for emergent readers use books containing eight to twelve pages of text, with one to three lines of text on a page. As children progress along the literacy continuum, they use longer books with more text on a page.

Instructional fiction texts are fresh and 90–95 percent familiar to the children who are to read the book. Fresh means the children have not previously seen, heard, or read the book. Familiar means the children have a talking understanding of the concept. It also means they can read or work through 90–95 percent of the words in the book and can use 90–95 percent of the skills the book requires. For nonfiction books, because the content and structure frequently offer more challenge to readers, the percentage of familiarity of an instructional text increases, to 92–97 percent.

To ensure success, instructional texts need to do three things:

- build on what children already know
- provide practice with what children can already do
- offer opportunities for new learning

Building on what children already know and providing practice with what they can already do make up the 90–95 percent familiar part. The opportunities for new learning, or the unfamiliar portion, should not exceed 5–10 percent. This means instructional text is significantly easy— much easier than most people imagine.

If the children can read and understand the majority of the text, the teacher can teach less, which allows him or her to teach better. If the teaching is better, chances are that more of what is taught will be learned. If we teach less and better, and then provide immediate opportunity for application, the skill, vocabulary, or strategy will become assimilated more deeply and will be more automatically recalled and used in other situations. Additionally, if the children can read and make sense of the text without struggling, more of their cognitive powers will be freed up to allow them to think.

Books written for guided reading instruction have four design features:

- **supports,** which keep children reading
- **challenges,** which keep children working
- **teaching points,** which keep children learning
- **talking points,** which keep children thinking

Supports are those features that make a book familiar to the reader. Challenges are the opposite of supports. These are places in the text where the teacher must slow down and teach or prepare the readers to encounter the challenge. Challenges frequently become teaching points. Teaching points are the specific skills, vocabulary, and strategies that will be taught and learned during the lesson. Talking points occur in text or illustration, and are places for readers to stop and think. Talking points are opportunities for comprehending skills to be addressed.

PREEMERGENT AND EMERGENT STAGES

Typically-developing children at the preemergent and emergent stages of literacy development are generally in prekindergarten, kindergarten, or first grade. These children are learning what language can do and how to make it work for them. Emergent children are beginning to learn how to read in guided reading lessons, using strategies to problem solve through words. Traditional text levels for these stages of development were known as readiness books and the first of several preprimers.

Concepts and content for children who are learning how to read include concrete concepts, objects, experiences, and actions familiar to young children. Language, vocabulary, and word study at this stage of development involve the structure of oral language, such as short sentences. Rhyme and word families and simple adjectives such as color and number words and "big" and "little" are the fodder of texts for children beginning to learn to read.

Illustrations are a primary source of information at these stages of development. The illustrations need to be done in a somewhat simple, straightforward style, with enough detail to link tightly with the print as too much detail might distract the reader. The artist's technique is another consideration. Light, pastel, and ephemeral styles of illustration have their place, but in general, more solid, realistic images offer better support and require less interpretation.

Sentence types and structures in text for children at these very beginning stages of literacy development include labels, captions, phrases, and very short sentences. Sentences that are complete on a page, not continuing across to the next page, are supportive. Repetition of a sentence stem or whole sentence throughout the text is a major support for very beginning readers. A single change within a sentence is enough of a challenge. The type of word that changes and the placement of that change are considerations. For example, nouns or verbs might change on each page, but only if the changing element is the middle or last word in the sentence. The word that changes should be depicted clearly in the illustration.

Text layout for these youngsters is a major concern. One or two lines of print, situated in the same place—at the top of each page or at the bottom of each page—supports preemergent and emergent children as they operate on text in an instructional setting. As mentioned previously, the most emergent children benefit from encountering a full sentence on a page, rather than a sentence that is strung over two pages or even through the whole book. The font needs to be of sufficient size with enough white space between the letters, words, and lines. The print should be placed on a white or light-colored background to ensure that the children can discriminate each letter, word, and line from the next.

Consider the type of text that is appropriate for preemergent and emergent readers. Texts that address concrete items and familiar actions offer a secure platform for making meaning. Label books do just that; each page of text serves as a label of one or two words that directly identify or explain the accompanying photo or illustration. A label format allows limited text with a direct link to the photographs—the kinds of features that support a very beginning reader. The first word generally repeats in two-word labels, which offers significant support, while the second word, generally a noun or verb, matches the image and helps give meaning to the words. Large font on a white field with ample white space, and consistent placement at the center of the right-hand page, are ideal for young, very beginning readers.

The sample from *The Giant's Breakfast* (Sample 6.1) illustrates the type of text appropriate for emergent readers. The ideas of a giant and types of breakfast foods may be familiar to many, if not most, children. The phrase "fe-fi-fo-fum" may be book language, but it is known to many children within the context of giants. The text includes the sight word "I." The word "smell" lends itself to being used in the conversation while the teacher is setting the scene as part of the guided reading teaching sequence (see Chapter 8). Also, the content words dealing with breakfast foods are fairly closely matched with the illustrations. The illustrations are clear and fairly precise, without extraneous detail. The first line repeats on each page, as does the stem of the second sentence. The only change is the noun at the end of each sentence. As discussed earlier, the noun change on each page is depicted in the illustrations. The print, of adequate size, appears at the bottom of each page on a white field with enough light between letters, words, and lines.

Sample 6.1

Fe-fi-fo-fum!
I smell oranges.

2

Fe-fi-fo-fum!
I smell oatmeal.

3

EMERGENT AND EARLY STAGES

Typically-developing emergent children can be found in prekindergarten, kindergarten, and first grade. Typically-developing early children are generally found in first and second grade. (Emergent and early children may show up in any grade, however.) Children at these stages of development are beginning to learn to read and continuing to learn to read, and are adding strategies to their word-working inventory. Traditional instructional texts for these children included one or more preprimers and primers.

Guided reading books for students at these stages need to continue to present objects, experiences, and actions familiar to young children. Texts with predominantly oral language structures still support these readers. Even more sight words carry them through these texts, and additional adjectives enrich these simple texts. Onomatopoeia-sound words like "ping, ping," "munch, crunch," and so on frequently add dimension to the text while being fairly workable.

Illustrations at this level include photographs and artwork that offer a moderate to high level of support, since pictures are still a primary source of information for cross-checking with the print. Labels and captions in nonfiction texts are of importance to the emergent and early reader. Attention to expository features such as table of contents, index, and glossary is initiated at the emergent stage of development.

Early readers have greater self-monitoring capability, and can therefore handle more than one repeating sentence pattern. The repetition in cumulative text subtly increases the amount of text without adding an inordinate amount of new text. Noun, verb, and adjective changes may occur at the beginning, middle, or end of the sentence. Opening or closing sentences may vary.

Early readers are prepared for varied placement of print on a page. In other words, early readers will scan the page for the location of the print when it is at the bottom on one page and at the top on the next. Early readers are good trackers of print. This allows them to read print that stretches over adjacent pages. These children are intrigued by and appreciate the use of speech and thought bubbles.

The sample from *Worms* (Sample 6.2) demonstrates the type of text appropriate for early readers. The type of illustration seen here is called landscape since it spreads over the two adjacent pages. These types of illustrations offer readers a panoramic view that allows the eye to seek ample detail. The text in this particular book contains one sentence stretched throughout. Notice how the two lines of text on each page are encapsulated to force the return sweep and thus prevent children from reading each line straight across.

Sample 6.2

Some worms went wiggling

into the ground and through the dirt,

The inviting illustration style enables the reader to use details in the picture to figure out the words. For example, words like "dirt," "soil," and "ground" may be used to discuss where the worms are. Children will use those words from their language to cross-check with the words in the text. They will try one word from their schema and see how well the way it sounds matches up with the way it looks. The same is true for the word "through," which can be hard on the eye, with the "-ough" in it. The worms that are entering the tunnels can be thought of, and talked about, as going "through the dirt."

A gradual increase in text scaffolds increasing fluency. While more text offers more opportunities for early readers to practice the strategies they have learned as emergent readers, supports such as repetition and a fairly close picture-text match with an appropriate, uncluttered, context continue to ensure success. Frequent use of sight words and familiar nouns and verbs provides ample support, which allows for increasing confidence. Supportive text frees cognitive energy for using strategies to ferret out new vocabulary.

EARLY AND NEWLY FLUENT STAGES

Early readers are practicing being readers. They practice strategies and self-monitoring behaviors. These are children who are self-monitoring and making their way through more and more new words with greater and greater alacrity. As for newly fluent readers, since they now can read, the focus is on helping them to comprehend as they read. Reading instruction for them shifts to understanding the author's message. This is comprehending beyond self-monitoring. Generally, newly fluent children are second and third graders, although children at this stage of development may pop up in any grade level. These children are reading longer picture books and short, simple chapter books that have more fully developed plots and more print on the page.

These readers are generally more mature than younger children. This means they can appreciate and understand the vagaries of certain types of fantasy and imaginative events in some genres. They can deal with abstract concepts and themes such as envy, catastrophes, courage, and so on. Newly fluent readers are prepared to process more information and subtle details about familiar objects and actions.

Since these children have had more experience with print, they have grown into the language of books. Newly fluent readers move smoothly between the comfort of oral language and the structures of written language. In addition, they enjoy and benefit from more descriptive language, including metaphors, similes, alliteration, onomatopoeia, and so on. Newly fluent readers are capable of working through more content vocabulary, and they rise to the challenge of locating definitions and explanations.

Because readers at this stage of development are attending more to the print, illustrations serve other purposes. They need not tie so closely to the text as they do for emergent and early readers. Illustrations for newly fluent readers might contain additional details that serve as subtle, embedded delights that become talking points for inference and prediction. Newly fluent children attend more closely to figures, maps, and graphs in nonfiction texts. These types of illustrations must be clear, specific, and of large enough scale to be easily interpreted. In addition, these graphics should be well labeled and captioned.

Newly fluent children are reading more fully developed stories. Such stories take more room to tell, so typefaces are smaller and there is less white space. Children at this stage of development can handle more text on a page—perhaps even a full page of text if the font is not too small. Text layouts with alternating pages of full print and illustration provide a balance for these readers.

Examples of texts for newly fluent readers include *Half for You and Half for Me* (Sample 6.3) and *The Night Queen's Blue Dress* (Sample 6.4). These books have more text and more fully developed and complex plots. Some books for newly fluent readers are broken into chapters and some are not. *The Night Queen's Blue Dress* is a chapter book. *Half for You and Half for Me* is not, but it can be broken into chapters by children with the teacher's help (see Chapter 9). Besides books like these, poems and short stories can be used with readers at this level.

The gradual increase of text and sophistication of concept continues along the continuum. Nonfiction books are appropriate for readers at any stage of development. Content-specific books for newly fluent readers may contain detailed scientific, technical information and content vocabulary. Many times expository language, such as "precipitation," is rough on the eye. The Latin and Greek roots of many scientific words and the complex phonemic combinations of some proper nouns make some words difficult to work through. A number of words have multiple meanings depending on the context. Words understood in one context may appear unfamiliar or are misunderstood when encountered in a different or scientific context. For example, the word "bridge," which may be a noun or a verb, may mean a span over a body of water, the command post on a ship, a card game, a dental appliance, or a part of the nose and may be cumbersome when used in nonfiction contexts. To read with understanding, and to continue to do so without becoming exhausted or sliding into shallow understanding, the reader must be secure and automatic in the use of strategies.

Sample 6.3

Raj and Han were brothers, and they liked to share things whenever they could.

"Half for you
and half for me," they said.

Then one day
Raj became greedy.

He began to cheat Han.

Sample 6.4

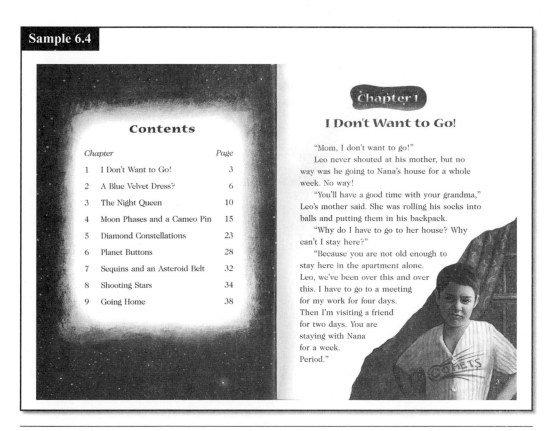

Contents

Chapter		Page
1	I Don't Want to Go!	3
2	A Blue Velvet Dress?	6
3	The Night Queen	10
4	Moon Phases and a Cameo Pin	15
5	Diamond Constellations	23
6	Planet Buttons	28
7	Sequins and an Asteroid Belt	32
8	Shooting Stars	34
9	Going Home	38

Chapter 1

I Don't Want to Go!

"Mom, I don't want to go!"

Leo never shouted at his mother, but no way was he going to Nana's house for a whole week. No way!

"You'll have a good time with your grandma," Leo's mother said. She was rolling his socks into balls and putting them in his backpack.

"Why do I have to go to her house? Why can't I stay here?"

"Because you are not old enough to stay here in the apartment alone. Leo, we've been over this and over this. I have to go to a meeting for my work for four days. Then I'm visiting a friend for two days. You are staying with Nana for a week. Period."

NEWLY FLUENT AND TRULY FLUENT STAGES

Newly fluent readers are learning how to think as they read. Truly fluent children read well and have learned to think on the fly as they read. Reading instruction for children at this stage is designed to take them higher in their thinking and deeper in their understanding. Generally, typically-developing fluent readers show up in third or fourth grade, but they may also show up later. Therefore, these children are usually older, if not more mature, than typical beginning readers.

Fluent children read chapter books and short novels with multidimensional characters; full, rich plots; and various settings. Stories might deal with even more abstract concepts and themes. Instruction might attend to the various motifs within different genres. Children at this level enjoy the chance to wrangle with literary language such as idioms, figures of speech, dialects, colloquialisms, and so on. Complex and compound sentences make up a portion of the text, with little or no repetition. Books for these children often lack illustrations. If they do have art, the pictures are few and may reflect mood rather than detail, or may serve as page fillers. Nonfiction texts at this level offer more detailed maps, line drawings, and various types of graphs.

The Newbery Honor Book, *What Jamie* by Carolyn Coman, is a good example of fiction text for truly fluent readers. The book is about fear of, and surviving with, the people who love you—pretty sophisticated, abstract ideas. The author shows the story, rather than telling it. It is the teacher's job to ensure that the kids "get it." ("It" being the concept of the story; "it" being recognition that the author is showing rather than telling; "it" being the imagery, word choice, pace, rhythm, tone, voice—everything that is the craft and skill that make this literature.)

Readers of this text need to be able to conjure up the pictures and shift them around to follow what the author intended, using their own schemas as the sieve to sort the words into images. Readers of this kind of text need to be strong and mature. They need to have lived long enough and to have held on to the experiences they have had and be prepared to use what they have lived to give life to the story that waits between the covers of the book. These readers must be truly fluent.

Reading at this level is about understanding. Nonfiction texts for truly fluent readers contain ample information, longer sentences, full paragraphs, and layers of meaning. Like fiction books, nonfiction books for truly fluent readers require the reader to weigh the text against the content of his or her own schema.

I guess it can be said that there are no bad books. Some children are considered to be struggling readers when in actuality they are struggling to read a book that is too hard. Ever try to pull on a pair of jeans two sizes too small? What happens? You get frustrated, sweaty, angry, and then quit, kick them off, and go get ice cream. Well, those struggling readers feel the same way.

Deciding which is the best book for each group requires a bit of science. The scientific elements that make up each book are summarized in Tables 6.1 and 6.2.

Table 6.1 identifies a few of the obvious features that place a book within an expected range. The plus sign following kindergarten and Grades 1 and 2 indicates the realization that children in middle and upper grades may be reading significantly below grade level. Just because he or she is in fourth grade doesn't mean a child can read traditional fourth-grade materials. When looking at factors such as page count and lines per page, keep in mind that word choice (vocabulary), sentence type and length, writing style, level of conceptual abstraction, and other aspects of text may influence the appropriateness of a book. Just because it's short doesn't mean it's easy.

Table 6.2 describes the nuances of the aspects that make a text what it is. Subtleties such as those described in Table 6.2 are often overlooked when analyzing a book. The first column contains information about grade level, guided reading (GR) level, Reading Recovery® (RR) level, and traditional basal level. Perhaps Tables 6.1 and 6.2 will assist when looking at potential books.

Table 6.1 Some Obvious Features That Place a Book Within an Expected Range

Grade Level	Stage of Development	Instructional Practice	Guided Reading Level	Text Page Count	Text Density
K+	Preemergent, emergent	Shared reading, guided reading	A, B	8, 9	1, 2 lines per page
1+	Emergent	Guided reading	B, C, D	8, 9	2–4 lines per page
1+	Early	Guided reading	D, E, F, G	8–12	3–6 lines per page
2+	Early	Guided reading	H, I, J	12–24	6–12 lines per page
2–8	Newly fluent	Transitional guided reading	J, K, L	24–36	Paragraphs; longer picture books
3–8	Newly fluent	Transitional guided reading	M, N, O, P	36–48	Short chapter books
4–8	Truly fluent	Reader's workshop, literature circles	Q, R, S	56–72	Chapter books
	Truly fluent	Literature circles, book clubs	T, U, V	80–120	Novels

Table 6.2 Summary of Considerations for Selecting Texts

	Grade and Level	Concepts and Content	Language Vocabulary, and Word Study	Illustrations	Sentences and Structure	Text Layout
PreEmergent-Emergent (Role Play and Experimental)	**Grades K, 1** GR level A–C RR level 1–4 Readiness–PP1	Concrete concepts, objects, experiences, and actions familiar to young childern	Oral language structures; some sight words; rhyme and word families; only adjectives are "big," "little," and color and number words	Supportive pictures with enough detail; link tightly with the text	Labels, captions, phrases, very short sentences; ample repetition; one noun or verb change at end or in middle of sentence	Consistent placement of text; one or two lines of print per page; whole sentence on one page; large type; ample white space between words and sentences
Emergent-Early (Early)	**Grades 1** GR level D–G RR level 5–12 PP1–Primer	Familiar concepts, objects, experiences, and actions	Predominantly oral language structures; more sight words; more adjectives; some onomatopoeia	Pictures that provide moderate to high support even in nonfiction	Repetition of two to three sentence patterns; noun, verb, adjectives may change; changes may occur at beginning, middle, or end of sentence; opening or closing sentences may vary; cumulative text	More varied placement of print; use of speech and thought bubbles; text may spread over adjacent pages; simple expository features; table of contents, glossary, index, captions, and callouts
Early-Newly Fluent (Transitional)	**Grades 1, 2** GR level H–M RR level 13–20 Books 1, 2	Some fantasy and/or imaginative events within familiar experiences; more detail about familiar objects and actions; more abstract concepts	Both oral and written language; more descriptive language: metaphor, alliteration, onomatopoeia, simile; more content-specific language	Pictures may include extraneous detail; may offer moderate support; maps, graphs, line drawings in nonfiction	Longer sentences, repetition of three or more sentence patterns; longer, more complex refrains; dialogue; beginning paragraphing	More text; perhaps full pages of text alternating with full-page illustrations; smaller type, less white space
Newly Fluent-Fluent (Independent)	**Grades 2+** RR level 20+	More fantsy; more abstract concepts; more complex plots; multiple and more complex characters	Literary language; expository language	Few illustrations; pictures reflect mood rather than detail; detailed maps, graphs, line drawings	Compound, complex sentences; little if any repetition; paragraphs	Full pages of text; chapters
Fluent-Proficient (Advanced)	**Grades 2/3+** RR level 25+	Genre specific; elaborate plots; complex episodes and events	Literary language; unusual, varied, and challenging vocabulary; rich descriptions	Few if any pictures; complex expository illustrations	Various sentence types	Full pages of text

Part III

Putting It All Together

Chapter Seven

Before Guided Reading

CHAPTER OVERVIEW

For many children, the first formal exposure to school is kindergarten. Traditionally, kindergarten is for language and social development, although in many places around the country kindergarten is beginning to look like a junior first grade. So is guided reading done in kindergarten? The answer to that question is like the answer to most other questions: it depends.

The truth is, guided reading is a rigorous instructional practice. Children need control of certain literacy behaviors in order to benefit from guided reading. Children must:

- have control of the concepts of print
- know the names of most of the lowercase letters
- know the sounds we give most of the lowercase letters and letter combinations
- know some sight words, including environmental words
- show continuing phonemic awareness
- have about fifteen minutes of "bottom power"

Most typically-developing children are at the preemergent stage of development when they enter kindergarten. These children are learning how the language works. Part of learning how language works involves the first five of those six behaviors.

In this chapter, we look more closely at literacy behaviors. We then look at three important types of activities that set the stage for guided reading:

- shared reading
- bridging practices
- small-group skill work

Finally, we consider the question of when to start guided reading in kindergarten, and examine some special considerations for using guided reading at this level.

LITERACY BEHAVIORS

Concepts of Print

Every written language is expressed in certain formats. To read a written language, one needs to know how it works on paper. Readers need to know how to handle the medium on which the language is written, whether it is a scroll, a book, or a screen. They need to know where the message comes from—print or picture. Readers need to know where to start and how to progress through the print. Children learn how to be with books at home and in preschool and kindergarten.

Letters and Sounds

As noted in Chapter 3, English is a code-based system. The code is made of symbols (letters) and values (sounds). Letters themselves do not have sounds. (Actually, they have many, which can be troublesome.) The reader or speaker gives the letters sounds. The sound we give a letter depends on its placement in the word. In order to benefit from guided reading lessons, children need to know the names of most, though not all, of the lowercase letters and the sounds we give to most, though not all, of the letters and letter combinations.

Sight Words

Children come to school having experienced many informal literacy events. Life is awash with print on food packages, stop signs, names of shops, and so on. When these signs have affective meaning for the child, the significance of the sign increases. Interaction with the child over the sign and its meaning increases the likelihood that the child will assimilate the word and its meaning. Frequently, the sight words a child brings to kindergarten are the words the child reads within his or her environment. Traditional lexical sight words (for example, *the*, *is*, and *and*) make their way into the child's literate field as he or she encounters them in formal and informal literacy events during the kindergarten day. (See Chapter 3 for more information on sight words.)

Phonemic Awareness

Phonemic awareness is one's ability to hear smaller and smaller units of sound within a linguistic stream. How many young children ask, "Who's Richard Stands?" or "What's a which-it?" after reciting the Pledge of Allegiance? We see evidence of phonemic awareness when a child first realizes that "ellemmennohpee" (l-m-n-o-p) is not the biggest letter in the alphabet. A child's ability to recognize, distinguish, discriminate, and provide rhyme also indicates his or her level of phonemic awareness. Phonemic awareness continues to develop through the years. First graders often think "once-upon-a-time" is a compound word. We all know about the abundant use of "doe wanna" and "na gonna" ("don't want to" and "not going to").

An example of how we use phonemic awareness is seen in a commercial for a cell phone. A guy with a phone to his ear says rapidly into the phone, "Canyouhearmenow?" He pauses, listens, and then says, "Good." How is it that we know exactly what he says when he utters, "Canyouhearmenow?" Several factors combine to help us make sense of what he says. The more experience we have with a language, the more its subtleties are imprinted on our brains. The high and low sound points that make the words that make up the sentence are familiar to those who have receptive control of a language. We know what those bits sound like and what they might mean when strung together. Then the context of using a cell phone and prior personal experience of not being able to hear well on a cell phone at times—perhaps even having asked a listener, "Can you hear me now?"—contribute to give meaning to the event. Understanding what the sounds mean and using the context enable us to understand on several levels.

In order to discriminate the separate sounds that make up a word, a child's ear needs to be tuned to hear the distinct units of sound. This is why kindergarten is generally full of rhymes, songs, chants, and pointing to words in big books with fingers, pointers, and voice. Phonemic awareness is a critical element of literacy development if a child is going to be able to encode and decode words.

Bottom Power

Bottom power is different from attention span. Young children can demonstrate amazing attention span. We've all seen young children play with blocks or paints for almost an hour. Generally, this occurs in situations where it is their idea—they chose to play and became engrossed in that play. Guided reading, however, is generally not the children's idea. To benefit from guided reading, children need to sit and participate in an experience that was not their idea. Guided reading is a focused, direct instructional experience with a lively pace directed by the teacher. Guided reading lessons for emergent readers last about fifteen minutes, perhaps as few as ten. When the children are done, the teacher is done too. Remember, the mind quits before the bottom rises.

Acquisition of Literacy Behaviors

So how do we ensure that these six behaviors make their way into kindergarten children's literate fields? We do what we've always done—sing, play with letters, read books, read big books, listen to stories on tape, write, read what was written, play—and we do it over and over again.

SHARED READING

Shared reading is the precursor to guided reading. Shared reading can be done with the whole class or a smaller group. Generally, some sort of enlarged text is used, most often a big book. Shared reading builds basic fundamental literacy elements such as:

- concepts of print
- speaking and reading vocabulary
- skills: letter names, letter sounds, blending
- sight words

Moving through a big book over several days in shared reading establishes a routine that sets the stage for the teaching sequence in guided reading, while bringing each of the children to a high degree of engagement. Children learn that talk precedes reading and that the talk makes the reading easier and more fun. The children learn that talking through the picture helps the reader know what the story is about. They realize that knowing what the story is about helps with the reading and enables the reader to make sense of the story. They learn that every book has a cover with an illustration. As they talk about the author and illustrator, they learn that books contain words and pictures that are made by people. This is important, since it leads to the realization that they too can be authors and illustrators.

BRIDGING PRACTICES

Children transition from the comfort of whole-group language and concept learning in shared reading to the rigors of small-group guided reading through bridging practices. In general, bridging practices build upon the language, concept, vocabulary, and skill learning that take place in shared reading. Small copies of the big book are used to engage children in small-group work.

These practices move children from a high degree of teacher support and whole-group community meaning building toward more structured, focused, and specific vocabulary and word work in a small group. They allow children to engage comfortably and attend closely to the letters and sounds, the sense of the sentences, and the ways the pictures relate to the text. Each of these is a rudimentary strategy that deals with several of the sources of information—graphophonic, syntactic, and semantic.

Bridging practices are more intimate, since they are small-group interactions. This allows the teacher to more precisely coach, question, and prompt the readers as they engage with the small copy of the big book. In addition, they allow the teacher to assess each child's literacy development more accurately.

Several types of small-group bridging practices ease children toward guided reading. You will notice that none of them is anything new. There is nothing new under the sun. The purpose of distinguishing these events is to elevate their value and point out the specific types of learning that result from them.

Types of Bridging Practices

Bridging practices include various independent and small-group interactions with small copies of the now familiar shared reading book. Children might listen to an audiotape of the story at a listening center. Each child should have a copy of the book to follow along and perhaps read along. The teacher might sit with a group of children, each with a copy of the book, reading to and with the children, discussing the details of illustration, pointing out the fine points of words, and examining punctuation. The teacher might use chart paper or a whiteboard to take words off the page of the book to isolate the specifics of word construction. It is important to note that the duration of these interactions is determined by the children's interest and bottom power. These should be happy, fun events.

Children might play school in small groups, using the big book and small copies. Here they might read to each other using the print, pictures, or memory. Pairs of children might read to each other. Kindergarteners might read to preschool children if some are present. Children are intrigued with hearing their own voices. Allowing the children to tape-record themselves reading is valuable on several levels. Affectively, it is a hoot for the children as they get used to hearing their own voices. Cognitively, the children will recognize what their reading sounds like and will better be able to compare what they are doing with the accurate model the teacher provides. The children will read and track the print or story line using their own audiotapes, which will serve as indicators of fluency.

Children can also read to a stuffed animal, to a photograph of someone, or to themselves in a mirror. A mirror attached to the lower part of a wall, near the floor, provides an "audience" of self to read to. A pillow on the floor in front of the mirror is a prime place for a child to be a reader. Several engaging sites can be established by positioning mirrors and pillows at different places around the edge of the classroom.

The teacher might provide a pocket chart with sentence strips, each with a sentence from a big book. The children can put the sentence strips in order in the pocket chart using the book as a guide. Later on, the children might use individual word cards to rebuild the sentences from the story.

Children might use highlighter tape to find and mark certain types of words in the book, such as color words or rhyming words. They might then place a sticky note on the margin to indicate the page where a word was found and marked. Able children might even copy the marked word onto the sticky note. These play activities are preludes to study skills that will come later.

Using letter tiles or magnetic letters to remake certain words found in the book draws attention to the fine points of word work. The words might then be copied into a blank book or onto small cards for the child's own use. These types of events move children from the broad experience of reading and hearing a story to the finer elements of words, letters and sounds, and punctuation. This leads to small-group skill work, another sort of kindergarten literacy work that prepares pre-emergent readers and continues to prepare some emergent readers for guided reading.

SMALL-GROUP SKILL WORK

Small-group skill work involves a teacher and a group of children investigating specific concepts, aspects of language, types of vocabulary, and literacy skills that are not necessarily related to a big book. The teacher might work with three or four children for five to ten minutes on skills such as the following:

- letter names
- word families
- letter sounds
- concepts of print
- encoding
- letter formation
- decoding
- sight words
- blending
- phonemic awareness
- interactive writing
- giving dictation
- taking transcription

Everything we do in kindergarten thickens children's literacy fields. Each of the engagements prepares children with the fundamentals of literacy that enable them to continue making and maintaining meaning from print. Some kindergarten children will progress from the pre-emergent to the emergent stage of development. The question again arises: Is guided reading done in kindergarten? And again, the answer is: It depends.

GUIDED READING IN KINDERGARTEN

When to Start

In kindergarten, guided reading begins with one homogeneous group of three or four children who:

- demonstrate sufficient bottom power
- have the concepts of print in place
- know most of the letters and most of the sounds
- know some sight words

A homogeneous group of kindergarteners may demonstrate these prerequisite behaviors in the second semester in half-day programs. Full-day programs often provide more time in a literacy-rich environment. Full-day kindergarten children may ripen earlier in the school year.

The temptation to start a group when three children demonstrate the required behaviors is great. However, it is recommended that the teacher wait for a fourth child to pop up, for two reasons. First, a group of three does not provide an adequate dynamic for instruction. Second, the children are only five years old. They need to spend their time playing and singing, getting their literacy pools filled up by more informal means.

Adapting the Rules

The rules for guided reading are different when guided reading is done in kindergarten. The usual process is described in detail in the next chapter, but for now, let's take a quick look at what is usual and use that standard as a basis for discussing how things differ in kindergarten. Generally, in a guided reading lesson, the following rules apply.

- One eight-page book per lesson is used.
- The lesson lasts fifteen to thirty minutes.
- All five steps of the teaching sequence make up one lesson.
- Children have three, four, or five lessons each week.

The same books used for emergent readers are used with kindergarteners, the first levels of these books being appropriate for new emergent readers. The books may be label or caption books, with one line of print and a repeating pattern. (See Chapter 6 for details on analyzing texts.)

Lessons in kindergarten may be shorter since the children are prime for a shorter amount of time. Lessons may last seven to ten minutes or more. All decisions are based on the children's behavior, however. It can happen that lessons later on in the year may last longer.

Because lesson times are shorter, steps of the teaching sequence (described in Chapter 8) may have to be spread over two days. Setting the scene and the picture walk generally go together in one lesson. The very next day the group meets, and after a quick warm-up talk and glance through the book, the children and teacher complete the lesson with the oral read and the return to the text. A formal response, the fifth step of the lesson, is generally omitted in kindergarten lessons except for the rereading over the coming days. As the lessons increase in length over time, the steps of the lesson might be completed in one sitting.

Kindergarten children have so many events available to them in the course of a school day. Guided reading might be viewed as a perk and done only once or twice a week initially, or three times a week later on. This allows time for other kinds of language and social learning that prepare children for the next twelve years and life after that.

It is important to note that once guided reading becomes a part of the kindergarten day for some children, shared reading does not stop. At no time does guided reading take the place of shared reading. Kindergarten children still need to experience the comfort and sense of community meaning making that shared reading provides. Shared reading continues to spackle the shallow spots in the literacy field of developing readers—in fact, shared reading needs to continue through all the grades for all children.

Chapter Eight

Guided Reading

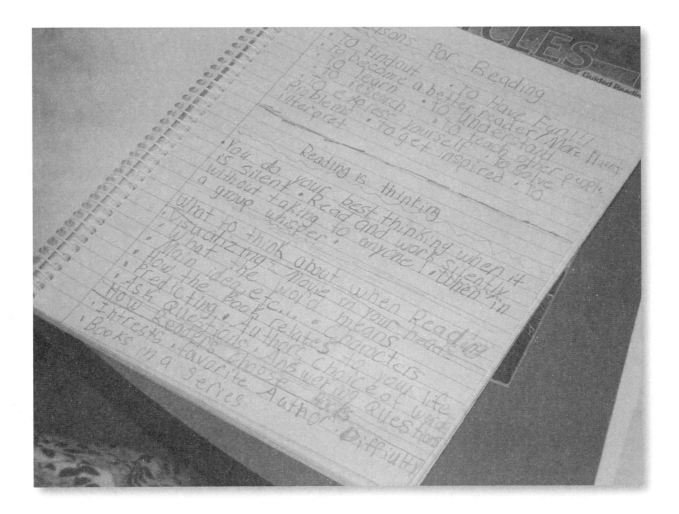

CHAPTER OVERVIEW

In this chapter, we begin with a quick review of the essential foundations for guided reading, which were laid out in detail in Parts I and II of this book:

- How learning happens (Chapter 1)
- Developmental stages and when to teach guided reading (Chapter 2)
- Learning to read: strategies and self-monitoring (Chapter 3)
- Guiding the reading: teacher talk (Chapter 4)
- Grouping and scheduling (Chapter 5)
- Selecting texts (Chapter 6)

The guided reading teaching sequence is the main subject of this chapter. It consists of six steps:

- setting the scene
- book introduction
- picture walk
- verbal read
- return to text
- response

Like beads on a string, each step of the teaching sequence sets up the next step. These six steps form the core of guided reading as an instructional practice. They also form the core of instruction in transitional guided reading, which is the next practice for children who are reading but still learning how to think while reading.

Before plunging in, however, a reminder is in order: it is the learners who really drive guided reading. Every decision, in every lesson, is based on the literacy behaviors demonstrated by the children in the group. Who is in each group, how long they stay there, what the teacher says to keep them focused and thinking—all these things depend on the individuals who are the target of all this attention. At its most basic, guided reading is about their success.

FOUNDATIONS FOR GUIDED LEARNING

How Learning Happens

Just as attaching one step to another gets us somewhere when walking, attaching one bit of knowledge to another gets us somewhere when learning. Children construct understanding by attaching new information to what they already know and can use. The teacher plays an essential role in this process—usually he or she is the one who builds the scaffold that connects one bit of knowledge to the next. This scaffold consists of four types of information: concepts, skills, vocabulary, and strategies.

Because new information is attached to existing information, careful assessment is an important part of the teacher's role. In order to know what each child needs next, the teacher must determine the specifics of which concepts, skills, vocabulary, and strategies the children currently have control of and can use. Guided reading lessons are an intensely intimate form of interaction, which facilitates such evaluation. By carefully observing children as they operate on print during small-group lessons, the teacher can see what sources of information the children use or ignore as they read, and can use this insight to structure support for the next learning.

Developmental Stages and When to Teach Guided Reading

Through their behaviors, children demonstrate what they can use from all that they know. Their behaviors help us to determine their stage of development—how far they are along the literacy continuum. This continuum of development consists of six stages: preemergent, emergent, early, newly fluent, truly fluent, and proficient readers.

Guided reading is the instructional (and evaluative) practice for emergent and early readers, children who are beginning to learn how to read. It is part of a logical sequence of literacy instruction that begins with development of basic literacy behaviors in preemergent children. With guided reading, emergent and early readers first learn strategies for making meaning and then learn to self-monitor, or recognize when meaning is breaking down.

Typically-developing children are emergent and early readers in first and perhaps second grade. Some quickly developing kindergartners may be emergent and perhaps early readers. Slowly developing children may be emergent and early readers in Grades 3 and up. Children who are new to English, regardless of their age and grade level, may be preemergent, emergent, or early readers. No matter what the children's age or grade level, it is their literacy development that determines which instructional practice will benefit them. We must teach children at the level where they are, not where they should be. This means that teachers in kindergarten through at least sixth grade should know how to teach guided reading groups.

Learning to Read: Strategies and Self-Monitoring

Learning to read has two parts: learning to use strategies and learning to self-monitor. Emergent readers learn strategies—mental problem-solving actions needed to make meaning—by using information sources, or cues, in the text. The information sources used in reading include pragmatic cues, graphophonics, syntax, semantics, schemas, sight words, and human cues.

Once children learn how to integrate these information sources using strategies, they are able to recognize when the meaning breaks down. This is self-monitoring, and it is the first level of comprehending.

Guiding the Reading: Teacher Talk

In guided reading, the teacher does not read the book to the children, nor does he or she read it with the children. Together, the teacher and a group of students work their way through the book following an orderly sequence of steps, with the children ultimately reading the book by themselves with the teacher's support. The teacher's role is to guide the students' thinking—to focus their mental decisions so that they streamline their problem solving before, during, and after the reading.

The teacher's strongest tool for guiding the students is his or her voice. Teacher talk falls into three categories: coaching statements, questions, and prompts. All three types can impact either inquiry processes or metacognitive processes. Teacher talk that triggers inquiry processes takes readers into information sources before and during reading. Metacognitive processes come into play during and after reading, and involve students in revisiting and reflecting on their own problem solving. This powerful aspect of teaching that results in learning is addressed in detail in Chapter 4.

Grouping and Scheduling

Guided reading involves a homogeneous group of four, five, or six children who know, use, and need to learn the same concepts, skills, and vocabulary. In a typical classroom, a teacher would form four groups, seeing three groups each day. Guided reading lessons run from fifteen to thirty minutes in length.

Scheduling lessons involves triagelike decision making. Emergent learners face more learning and have farther to go in their development, and frequently have limited bottom power, so emergent readers require shorter, more frequent lessons. Guided reading lessons for emergent readers might last fifteen to twenty minutes and there may be four or five of them each week. Lessons for early readers may last twenty to thirty minutes and there may be three or four each week.

Details of scheduling and keeping the others engaged are outlined in Chapter 5.

Selecting Texts

Guided reading lessons are conducted with a book selected by the teacher. Either fiction or nonfiction books may be used in guided reading lessons. Each group gets its own book. Generally, guided reading lessons for emergent readers use books with eight to twelve pages, with one to three lines of text on a page. Books for early readers contain more text and perhaps more pages.

The teacher selects a text that is fresh and familiar. Fresh means that the book has not been read, heard, or seen. Familiar means that the children in the group have a talking understanding of the concept, can read or work through 90–95 percent of the words, and can use 90–95 percent of the skills the book requires. This level of support builds upon the concepts, skills, and vocabulary the children in the group already know, while providing practice in using this knowledge. These two factors—building upon what is known and providing practice with what is currently used—render the book 90–95 percent familiar. In addition, the book needs to offer opportunities for new learning, or be 5–10 percent unfamiliar. Chapter 6 details the science of selecting books for instruction.

THE TEACHING SEQUENCE

Guided reading is a framework of interaction that weaves the routines of talk, assessment, observation, thinking, rethinking, more talk, and finally reading. This framework provides for a rhythm of communication between the teacher and children that results in learning. The teaching sequence is actually a shared dominance. The teacher, the children, or both dominate each step of the lesson. The cadence of this interplay of dominance over the text results in learning.

The purpose of the teaching sequence is to set the children up to read and understand the text by themselves with the teacher's support. Support comes in the form of teacher talk. At no time does the teacher read the book to the children, nor does the teacher read along with the children. If the book is the right one for the group, there should not be any need to read the book to the children. To do so would diminish the level of strategizing the children would do. If the teacher needs to read the book to the children for them to "get it," the book is too hard.

The teaching sequence has six steps:

1. setting the scene

2. book introduction

3. picture walk

4. verbal read

5. return to the text

6. response

Details of each step follow.

Setting the Scene

Introducing the book is a critical first step. The goal here is to alert the readers to the concept and relevant vocabulary without giving it all away. The teacher also tells the students why they will be reading this particular text. The reason might be to learn about a particular subject, or because the book is like another one the children have read about a subject, or just to enjoy the book. The children should know why they are dedicating time to this particular text.

The first step of the lesson is conversation that orients the children to the concept contained in the book. The teacher does not necessarily show the book to the children yet. Rather, the teacher tells the children what the book is about. Giving the children the concept, rather than having them guess in the name of prediction, streamlines their thinking. The teacher also tells the children that they know about the concept. He or she does not ask them, "Have you ever seen/gone/found . . .?" To do so serves only to alienate the child or children who may have not had the pertinent firsthand experience. Consider the inclusive power of the following exchange between a teacher and her group while setting the scene for *The Giant's Breakfast*, a book about smelling breakfast foods:

Teacher: You know about giants.

Child: Giants are very, very big.

Teacher: Yes, they are very big. You know what a giant says.

Child: I know! I know! Giants say, "Fee-fi-fo-fum."

Teacher: Yes, giants do say, "Fee-fi-fo-fum."

The concepts in this book are giants and breakfast foods. This first part of the conversation activates the areas of the children's brains that deal with giants and what they say. The teacher has told the children that they know about giants. She did not ask them if they have ever seen one. Certainly, at some point in their young lives, these children have had some encounter with a giant, whether it be on the screen, in a book, or on a can of peas.

In the "olden days," each story in the basal included a set of flash cards on which were written the words the children needed to know in order to read the story. Age-mates of mine might recall the practice of using those cards to introduce new vocabulary prior to the reading. We would hold up a card with a word on it and ask what it was; no one would know, so we'd tell them the word. The children would repeat the word each time when asked, "What's this word?" and "Say it again," and "One more time." Then the card would be placed in a pocket chart. On and on the cards would go, until the pocket chart held a series of words in a vertical list.

Next, just to make sure they knew the words, we would "whack the words." The teacher, with pointer in hand, would smack each word card and ask, "What's this word?" and the children would dutifully say each word. The real test of word knowledge came when the teacher would whack the words in random order!

Finally, it was time to read—and, of course, they didn't know the words. "How can you not know that word?" I asked one group in frustration. Of course, I was being rhetorical; however, being first graders, they didn't know that. So Bobby answered, "Because there's other words around it." Out of the mouths of babes, huh? Bobby stated the phenomenon called change of state where an object or person is not recognized outside the state in which it was learned. It makes perfect sense: the children learned the words as isolated units, in a vertical form, and then were asked to read them in a different state of existence: in a horizontal form, surrounded by other words. It's a wonder the species has continued.

Flash cards have no place in guided reading lessons. The teacher does not preteach the vocabulary. All specific skill and vocabulary instruction is done within the context of the talking, thinking, and reading.

In the preceding dialogue, the teacher brings what a giant says to the children's minds. This is helpful since "fee-fi-fo-fum" appears on nearly every page of the book. She does not prepare flash cards with those words in order to preteach the vocabulary. Rather, she pulls the relevant vocabulary from the children. So far, the children are having a successful encounter. The exchange continues:

Teacher: The giant in this book can smell things for breakfast. You know foods we eat for breakfast.

Children: Cereal! Scrambled eggs! English muffins! Pizza!

Teacher: Let's write some of these things on the board. Let's see, "Cereal."

The teacher writes some of the words on a chalkboard, dry-erase board, or chart paper. The teacher doesn't write only words that actually appear in print. The teacher writes what the children offer. The concept vocabulary—in this case, the names of breakfast foods—brings up relevant ideas and perhaps some of the words the children may meet in print. Setting the scene creates a niche for the story to fit within each reader's experience.

On occasion, the teacher may "float" vocabulary. Floating vocabulary is when the teacher uses certain words from the text in conversation. Floating vocabulary gets the words into the air around the group and then into their ears and their brains. The decision to float a word is made judiciously, since the purpose of setting the scene is to bring out from the children's minds that which will enable them to read and understand what the author has written. The teacher's job is to facilitate this process.

Book Introduction

The second step of the lesson is to introduce the book to the members of the group. Here, the teacher gives each child a copy of the book, with instructions to stay on the cover. Some teachers feel it is better if the teacher holds a copy of the book, to control page turning, and perhaps slyly covers up the text with one hand. This is fine, but if the objective is to have each child be a reader, then why not give each child a copy of the book? Children do learn the routine of the steps of the teaching sequence, and they will learn to stay on the cover.

After each child is given a copy of the book, the teacher reads the title and the author's and illustrator's names and then says something about them. If you don't know anything, make up something. Oh come on, we've all done it, use what you know—for example, for the book *The Giant's Breakfast*, you might say something like, "The author loves to write about food." That's enough for the children to begin to connect with the parents in the book as real people by helping them visualize these folks. Next, the teacher and children examine the details of the cover illustration, check out the back cover as sometimes good stuff sits back there, and then move to the title page if there is one. The discussion of these initial illustrations provides additional chances to investigate the concept. Since most books for emergent and early readers are short, they may lack access features such as a table of contents, index, or glossary. However, if the book does have a table of contents, that's the next stop.

In nonfiction texts, the table of contents is an outline of main ideas. The teacher guides the students in the reading of each section title, or just the section that will be read that day (you don't have to read the whole book), and the key word in each title is found. The page numbers are examined as well. Children need to learn to determine the length of a section, which may indicate the amount of information contained there. They also need to recognize the page number on which a section ends. Knowing the beginning and ending page numbers helps with working in the index. Emergent and early readers need to know what an index is, how it is organized, and where to look for an index. The index takes on a more prominent role in transitional guided reading lessons. In fiction, the table of contents may indicate the story map. Each section title may reflect a plot point or character.

Picture Walk

The third step of the lesson is to generally investigate each page of the book in a quick, purposeful manner. The purpose of the picture walk is to allow children to examine the illustrations as a source of information and use that information to check against another source. This process of using information from one source—the illustration—and checking it against another—the print—is the important strategy known as cross-checking. The teacher's role in this is to watch for cross-checking opportunities and use them for strategy building. Toe dipping is an example of cross-checking. Toe dipping is illustrated by the following conversation during the picture walk in *The Giant's Breakfast*:

Teacher: Look at page four. What do you see?

Child: He's making toast. Lots of toast.

Teacher: Yes, he is. Look on page five. What do you see there?

Children: Bacon! Pork chops!

Teacher: What is that? Find the word "bacon." Look fast.

At this point, the teacher has directed the children's eyes and minds to the print to search for the word "bacon." The children skim and scan, but don't actually read, the print for a word that fits the visual image of their aural image. In this case, the corresponding actual word on the page is "ham." Here's what happens:

Child: It ain't bacon.

Teacher: How do you know?

Child: None of the words has a "b" in it.

Teacher: Oh. Well, we'll figure out that word when we read it.

The teacher could pursue the investigation of the word, eventually working toward the accurate "ham." But accuracy is not the goal at this point. Right now, right here on this word, the children need to learn and use the strategy of cross-checking.

The purpose of toe dipping is to help children confirm or discount a prediction by using multiple sources of information. The strategy of cross-checking is a powerful one that increases the children's repertoire of tools. Strategy use builds their capacity to self-monitor, which is a prelude to accuracy, which feeds comprehending.

The picture walk may also be a time for examining and discussing features of print such as italics, speech bubbles, or letter or diary format. Likewise, it may be a time to attend to and analyze the details of words, such as the parts of compound words, prefixes or suffixes, various types of punctuation, alternative word choices, little words that can be found in big words, and so on. It is important to note, however, that the specific skill teaching occurs later in the lesson.

The Verbal Read

The fourth part of the lesson is perhaps the most important, but it is frequently the most misunderstood. The verbal read is the prime assessment opportunity in the lesson. This is where the teacher gets to watch and hear all of the children operate on this specific text. This is where the children's eyes and minds hit the page. The children execute strategies on a whole connected text.

The teacher directs the children to "read the whole story out loud for yourself and I'll watch and listen." Verbal reading is a homogeneous group of four, five, or six children reading the same text at the same time. The more homogeneous the group, the more together the reading should sound. In general, the children should be reading within a word or half-word of each other.

One of the advantages of verbal reading is that it enables the teacher to observe each child as he or she processes the same text the other children are reading. This allows the teacher to see how each child operates compared with the other children in the group. The makeup of the group sets the standard for behavior for each member of that group. The teacher can see whether someone is pulling ahead or falling behind. This is important, since homogeneous groups allow for streamlined teaching that ensures more learning.

In contrast, some teachers have the children stagger their reading. In other words, one child starts to read the first page. The teacher then taps the next child, who starts to read the first page. The teacher taps each child, one after the other in turn. The four, five, or six children each read the same text at slightly different times. The result is a cacophony of young voices. This form of verbal reading lessens the teacher's opportunities for assessment.

Verbal reading is not choral reading. Choral reading is rehearsed for the purpose of reading with one voice, as in a presentation. Nor is verbal reading round-robin reading. Round-robin reading is each child having a chance to read a segment of the text out loud alone, as was done in traditional reading lessons. Teachers liked round-robin reading, and many still do, because this way they can clearly hear each child. How nice for the teacher! What round-robin reading does for the children is fracture the reading experience. They read only a slice of a larger text. Of course, we want to believe that the children are each reading silently, comprehending fully as each of their groupmates takes a turn. In our heart of hearts, though, we know they are not. They are doing exactly what we once did when reading in a reading group. Some children are slyly peeking ahead to see how much or little they will have to read. Some are dreading their experience because it is too much, or worrying that they won't know some of the words. And others are silently whining because they don't get to read a lot. In other words, their brainpower is being wasted on all the things that have nothing to do with reading.

The verbal read is the ultimate assessment of teacher expertise. The verbal read is the proof of how well the teacher has formed the group, selected the text, introduced the book, and taught and supported strategy use. In addition, teacher expertise is needed to recognize, record, analyze, interpret, and then use each literacy behavior the children demonstrate as they read.

The teacher's role during the verbal read is to watch and listen to each child as he or she reads. The teacher makes note of observable behaviors that serve as evidence of which sources of information each child is using, integrating, or ignoring. Each decision the teacher makes is derived from the children.

When an error occurs, the teacher may decide to stop the group or an individual, or may decide to just let it go. This point of decision making is the truest test of the teacher's knowledge of each child's literacy development. Again, what the children do dictates the teacher's actions. For example, if a child substitutes a word that is semantically and syntactically correct, such as "pony" for "horse," the teacher has to decide whether to stop the child at that point of error or wait. Why would the teacher wait? Why not jump in and save the child or children from the abyss of inaccuracy? In an example like this one, when in doubt it is better to wait rather than intervene. Waiting allows the child an opportunity to self-monitor and perhaps self-correct.

Note Taking During the Verbal Read

In the verbal read, the teacher does not read to the children or along with them. In fact, the teacher needs to close her copy of the book and prepare to take notes. A number of methods exist for note taking during the verbal read. Using a notebook with pages tabbed with each child's name is one method. Another is to keep a pad of two-inch-square sticky notes with a cord laced through it as a tabletlike pendant. When the teacher notices a behavior to record, she writes the child's name and a note on the top sticky note, then folds it back to expose the next, clean sticky note ready for note taking. At the end of the day, the teacher peels off all the notes and places them in the children's assessment folders. A large desk calendar page with a child's name written in each two-inch-square block can also serve as a storage place for the individual sticky notes. At the end of the day, the teacher places each sticky note in its corresponding square. A different-color sticky-note pad pendant for each day alerts the teacher to the frequency of note taking for each child.

Another method of taking notes involves four-by six-inch index cards stagger-taped to a clipboard. The bottom edge of each card is exposed with a child's name written on it. As the teacher sees a behavior to be noted, she flips to that child's card and makes the note. This clipboard can be used throughout the day, not just during guided reading. A code can be established to identify the various events during the day when notes are kept. As with any form of informal assessment, dates are critical and automatically need to be added to each note.

These recording forms become succinct records of a child's performance. The information contained on the cards, sticky notes, or notebook pages enables the teacher to paint more accurate and honest portraits of a child's development. Report card narratives and parent conferences can then become detailed depictions of what a child knows and can do.

In the short term, notes taken during the verbal read provide immediate data for specific strategy, skill, and vocabulary teaching. The next step of the teaching sequence is where this direct, contextualized teaching takes place.

Return to the Text

When the verbal read is finished, each of the children has processed a complete, connected text. There are two reasons to return to the text: to teach the specific skills and vocabulary the book offers, and to metacognize the problem-solving strategies the children used or missed.

The text provides the fodder for explicit strategy, skill, and vocabulary instruction. After the verbal read, the teacher and children revisit this familiar text for several purposes. The teacher may have individuals or pairs of children read segments of text aloud. The teacher may recognize individual efforts at using strategies. He or she may have a child articulate specific problem-solving actions, and then discuss other problem-solving strategies to ensure metacognition. The teacher might coach, question, and prompt the children for use and integration of cues on troublesome words. The following represents a typical exchange between a teacher and a child who worked through a word.

Teacher: All of you all did such a good job reading this whole story. Jacob, I saw you working on a word on page four. Everyone, let's go back to page four. Jacob, you read page four for us.

Jacob: Fe-fi-fo-fum. I smell toast.

Teacher: Good reading. Which word did you work on?

Jacob: [Points to the word "toast."]

Teacher: What is that word?

Jacob: Toast.

Teacher: Right! How do you know it is "toast"?

Jacob:'   Cause it looks like toast.

Teacher: Yes, the picture looks like toast. You used the picture. What else told you that word is "toast"?

Jacob: I don't know.

Teacher: When you looked at the word, what did you do?

Jacob: I sounded it out.

Teacher: What did you do when you sounded it out?

Jacob: I sounded it out.

Teacher: I know, that is a good thing to do. Tell me what your eyes and mouth did as you sounded it out.

Jacob: I looked at the letters and figured it out.

Teacher: Yes, you did. You did good thinking. You saw a "t" at the beginning. Then I bet you saw the "st" at the end of the word. And you know that "oa" says the long "o" sound. Let's look at that word up here.

At this point, the teacher takes the word off the page, isolates it on the dry-erase board, and revisits the specifics of the sound and letter units that make up the word. The teacher teaches or reviews the strategy of reading into a word. This exchange shows how the teacher recognizes individual efforts while including all of the children in the group in the precise skill teaching.

The particular skills and vocabulary the book offers are taught and learned at this point of the lesson. Remember that the opportunities for new learning make up only 5–10 percent of the book. This factors into just a few specific skills or vocabulary items to work on. In other words, the teacher can teach less, teach it better, and provide immediate opportunities to use what has been learned, which means more gets learned and it lasts longer.

Responding to the Text

To ensure that the skills, vocabulary, and strategies addressed during the lesson make their way into the students' long-term memories and become automatically useable, the students need to revisit the text outside the lesson. The last step of the lesson offers children an opportunity to respond to the text. Five types of responses drive readers back into the text:

- verbal responses
- written responses
- image responses
- three-dimensional responses
- technological responses

The various types of responses tap into different intelligences, modalities, and learning styles, and allow students to express their understanding in multiple ways. Not every book requires a formal response beyond a discussion. Every book does involve some kind of verbal response, however.

Responses are events that children can engage in at their seats, when not in a group with the teacher. The children need to learn how to do each kind of response, and the standards of quality that apply.

Written Responses

Writing underscores each of the other types of responses. Questions need to be written when preparing to do a verbal response such as an interview. Titles and captions need to be written for image responses such as graphic organizers or illustrations. Titles, labels, and descriptions need to be written for three-dimensional responses. Text for PowerPoint presentations and shot lists for photos and videos need to be written for technological responses.

By themselves, written responses do not necessarily mean book reports. Short, focused writing exercises represent a more pointed response to what has been read. Examples of written responses include

- blurbs
- review statements
- speech or thought bubbles
- recaptioning
- headings and subheadings
- chapter titles
- footnote or sidebar explanations or definitions

The effectiveness and value of written responses frequently depend upon the fine motor control a youngster has, since penmanship and spelling prowess are developmental. Written responses might involve short, simple bits of writing, rather than long, involved events that diminish the act of reading.

Written responses to fiction text include having children write, or dictate, a blurb for the back cover of the book. A blurb is a three- or four-sentence inducement to read the book. A review statement is one or two lines about the book. Speech or thought bubbles are another type of simple written response appropriate to guided reading books. A child draws a speech or thought bubble on a two-by two-inch sticky note, which is then placed over a character's head in an illustration. The child determines what that character is thinking or saying and writes it in the bubble. Children enjoy this response, and it provides an opportunity for them to infer.

Longer picture books, those twenty-four-page books that are especially appropriate for transitional guided reading, can be broken into three or four chapters. Chapters break when a change of setting or action occurs. The teacher tells the children where the chapters break and demonstrates how to place an edge tab on the margin. (Edge tabs are sticky notes placed with the adhesive end on the margin and the rest hanging outside the book, so the book has a "hairy" look.)

Each chapter tab is placed slightly below the previous one so it can be easily seen when the book is closed. As each chapter is completed, each child writes a title for that chapter. A chapter title is a synthesis statement, synthesis being a comprehending skill. When the book is finished, children can compile the chapter titles into a table of contents.

Nonfiction written responses include captioning or recaptioning the illustrations. Captions are summary statements and are one or two sentences long. Summary statements tell who or what is involved, describe what happened, and end with a conclusion or deduction—both of which are comprehending skills. Finding and marking key words is a valuable study skill that counts as a written response. Once a key word is marked with transparent temporary highlighting tape, the child needs to copy the word and page number onto an edge tab. A page might have several key words and therefore several edge tabs. In addition, once a key word is found, it may be necessary to find the definition or explanation of that word within the text. The definitions or explanations can be marked in the same manner and copied or summarized on a sticky note and used as a footnote or sidebar. (Sidebars are footnotes attached to the outside margin.) Key words can then be compiled into an index or glossary and attached to the book.

Verbal Responses

It is natural for us to talk about what we have read. Verbal responses are just that: verbal. As a teacher, I prefer verbal responses to the others for several reasons. Verbal responses are immediate, authentic, unrehearsed, and subject to revision, and they are occasions for children to think on their feet. Not only that, the teacher has nothing to put in a bag, load into the backseat of the car, and drive home, only to leave it parked in the driveway overnight and drive it back to school in the morning. Examples of verbal responses include:

- discussion
- rereading
- tape-recording
- at-home reading
- acting out the story
- reader's theater
- book talks

Discussion can be of any kind—about the concept, author, illustrator's style, or literary elements contained in the book, such as characters, settings, or action. Rereading is another familiar verbal response. If chosen appropriately, the book should be independent at this point. Some teachers provide each group with a box or basket in which one copy of the book is placed following the lesson. The group then shares the contents of this box, reading to each other, reading into the tape recorder, or reading to stuffed animals (but not reading to children who are not in their group). The book can also go home once it has been read in a guided reading lesson. Children in the group can act out the book or share it as reader's theater. A book talk is another simple, effective verbal response.

Image Responses

Image responses enable children to rearticulate narrative information in a visual form. A number of types of image responses exist and can be used with fiction and nonfiction texts. Several will be discussed here:

- pictures
- book covers
- storyboards

- time lines
- Venn diagrams
- semantic grids
- webs

The most familiar type of image response is the plain old picture. Children read a story or text and then draw a picture. While this is a valid response to a text, too often the picture is just that: a picture—a superficial interpretation of what was read. Having children focus on the literary elements of character, setting, and plot increases the value of such a task. When appropriate, pictures should show evidence of protagonist and antagonist, and details of setting including dimensions such as weather, season, and so on, as well as obvious action. Pictures can be made in response to nonfiction texts as well. The details of the picture deal directly with the details of content and concept. This type of focused illustration clearly indicates that thinking has taken place.

Evidence of literary elements is also needed when children make a new book cover for the book. However, book covers can be made for nonfiction texts as well. Nonfiction covers focus on the content and related concepts addressed in the book. Emergent and early children can draw a front plate to remake a book cover. Longer picture books and short chapter books, such as those used in transitional guided reading with newly fluent children, offer even greater opportunity for details. Some book jackets include redesigned spine, front and back plates, and end flaps. Some of these book jackets can be quite involved and may include a blurb, a note about the author, and perhaps review statements. Such elements integrate written responses into the image response, thereby increasing its value.

The same kinds of detailed illustrations are used in construction of a storyboard. A storyboard is a series of pictures and brief texts that show the highlights of character, setting, and action in each chapter or segment of a book. Storyboards are generally used with fiction. Some chapters or segments might have more than one illustration. Four- by six-inch cards limit the illustration space and are thus ideal for getting a student to visually summarize the people, places, and plot points. A brief written summary highlights the "who" or "what," the "what happened," and a conclusion or deduction. A two- by four-inch sticky note works well for the written part because the space is limited and the sticky note can be attached to the bottom edge of the card it accompanies.

Image responses include various types of graphic organizers. Obviously, time lines are especially useful for sequencing events. Their value is realized in fiction and nonfiction texts. Venn diagrams compare and contrast two or three items. (Comparing and contrasting more than three items can be cumbersome in a Venn diagram and therefore they require a different vehicle.) Venn diagrams for fiction are used to compare and contrast characters within a story or between stories, or to compare or contrast different stories, authors, and so on. Venn diagrams for nonfiction texts are used to compare two or more of just about anything. For example, nonfiction Venn diagrams could display the similarities and differences between types of trees, animals, rocks, energy, and so on.

A semantic grid is used to compare, contrast, or display the traits of four or more items. Generally, the traits are listed across the top and the items to be discussed are listed along the left. Each item is considered against each trait, and a description or check mark is made in each cell aligned with the item and trait. Semantic grids display a lot of information in an orderly fashion. They can be used with fiction or nonfiction texts. Fiction examples include analyzing various versions of a story, such as the different accounts of the Cinderella story, or the same story written by a number of authors, or different parodies of the same tale. Nonfiction examples include comparing and contrasting the different features of different members of a group, such as trees or mammals or rocks.

Webs are familiar image responses that can be used with fiction or nonfiction. Webs are devices for organizing information that is being gathered or that has already been gathered. To be effective, however, webs need to have clearly defined cells. Cells are the subtopics identified by a ring around the topic, to which details are attached with short lines. Fiction webs can be used to organize the literary elements or the traits of the characters in a story. Nonfiction webs can organize the particulars of various features such as habitat, predators, reproduction, migration, and so on with animals, or the fine points of types of seed, leaf, life cycle, region, and so on with plants.

Three-Dimensional Responses

Traditionally, a three-dimensional response meant a diorama. Whoever thought this was a good idea? Too often a book is used because "then we can make a quilt." Reading a book is not a way to do a project. Consider ourselves—most of us are proficient readers. We have to read. When we have finished a delightful, quality read, is our first thought to get a shoebox and dolls? I hope not! What do we do when we have finished one of the wonderful books we relish? We talk about it. We tell someone what the book is about and why we liked it. We discuss the book to share what we know and feel about it. We don't make a diorama.

In general, a three-dimensional response involves a display, collection, or some sort of realia. Two such examples will be discussed here: the "book in a bag" and the "museum." When doing a book in a bag, children gather items, props, and artifacts that represent characters, settings, and plot points. The items are put into a bag and are then used as display items in a book talk, which combines the visual response with a verbal response. A silent version of this is a museum—the reader gathers up objects in the same way as for a book in a bag but displays them with placards that identify each item. One terrific example that I've seen displayed involved articles representing different folktales and nursery rhymes. For example, a scrap of wrinkled, dirty red cloth was displayed with a placard that read, "All that remains of Red Riding's hood." Three-dimensional responses are delightful alternatives to paper-and-pencil events. The kind of decision making used to choose one item over another taps into many types of thinking.

Technological Responses

Students today are living the George Jetson life, or so it seems. Need to load software? Call a six-year-old. System frozen? Get an eight-year-old. Can't read the note your daughter left because it is a series of two- and three-letter and number combinations? Welcome to the twenty-first century. In many fortunate school districts, classroom filmstrip projectors and even overhead projectors have been replaced with projection systems hung from the ceiling and controlled with a remote. Chalkboards were replaced with whiteboards, which were replaced with front-projection interactive plasma displays. Beam me up, Scotty!

Children today are so at ease with electronics that baffle adults that it is senseless for children to not use them. Most digital cameras take still photos and video, the Internet offers limitless access to everything imaginable and otherwise, and it all keeps on getting better and more confusing. (I feel so old!)

Technology, like writing, may underscore many of the other types of responses. Examples of technological responses include:

- videotaping an interview between a student interviewer and another portraying a character
- a video or photographic montage to accompany a three-dimensional display
- photographs to illustrate a written report
- PowerPoint presentations that include photos, video, animation, and/or sound effects

Chapter Nine

After Guided Reading

CHAPTER OVERVIEW

Guided reading is the instructional practice for children who are learning how to read—both emergent and early readers. We know that it is the instructional practice through which children learn the strategies that enable them to make the meaning and to self-monitor. What happens, though, when the children can read? Now what? Too often, in too many places, reading instruction stops. Once children look like they are reading, it is figured that they can read, and so let 'em read. If anything is done in the name of reading, it's the "novel," usually with the whole class.

Reading instruction for children who know how to read the words needs to shift to ensuring that the children understand what they are reading. For newly fluent and truly fluent readers, the instructional focus is on comprehension. The purpose of reading instruction at these stages of development is to take children higher in their thinking and deeper in their understanding. These instructional practices are designed to enable children to think on multiple levels while reading on the fly. These practices also deepen the reader's understanding of the content and the writer's craft.

This chapter discusses the details of three instructional practices that follow guided reading:

- transitional guided reading (for newly fluent readers)
- reader's workshop (for truly fluent readers)
- literature circles (for truly fluent readers)

These practices, along with others not discussed here, such as reciprocal teaching and book clubs, form a logical sequence—a hierarchy of sorts. In other words, each practice sets up the next instructional practice. Each teaching sequence enables the readers to move forward in their reading, to accept greater and different types of responsibility for the thinking and discussion involved.

TRANSITIONAL GUIDED READING

Transitional guided reading is the instructional practice for newly fluent readers who can read but may or may not comprehend what they are reading. This instructional practice serves three main purposes:

- It transitions the focus of instruction from making meaning to maintaining it by focusing on comprehension.
- It transitions the readers from oral reading to silent reading.
- It transitions the readers from short texts to longer picture books for building stamina.

Transitional guided reading is also called silent guided reading because it ties children's brains to the text so that they learn how to think about what they are reading silently. The teacher locates various types of comprehending opportunities in the longer picture books and uses them as talking points throughout the lesson. Reading skills, study skills, and vocabulary make up the teaching points in the lesson. Essentially, it is an instructional practice designed to ensure comprehension. The primary vehicle for ensuring comprehension is taking notes, one of several study skill opportunities provided by longer texts.

Groups

Newly fluent children are organized into homogeneous groups. The size of the group still numbers four to six children who know and use the same information, who read and think in the same ways. It is possible that a third-, fourth-, or fifth-grade classroom might have one guided reading group of emergent and early readers, one or two transitional guided reading groups of newly fluent readers, and perhaps a reader's workshop group or literature circle of truly fluent readers. The guided reading and transitional guided reading groups need to meet with the teacher at least three times in a week.

Texts

As discussed in Chapter 6, books used for transitional guided reading are longer picture books or short chapter books. Fiction books have more fully developed and complex plots. Nonfiction books contain more detailed scientific information.

Since the books contain more text, lessons may extend over several days, with a segment of the text read each day. Chapters form logical segments. Books that don't have chapters can be broken into chapters by the children with the teacher's help. Chapters break when a change of setting or action takes place in the book. Prior to the first lesson, the teacher marks the chapter breaks in his or her copy and then leads the children in marking the chapters in their books. Sticky notes placed in the margin so they hang out from the book are useful chapter markers. A chapter title can be written on the edge tab following the reading of the chapter. Chapter titles are a synthesis statement and serve as a comprehending skill.

Teaching Sequence

The teaching sequence used in transitional guided reading is based on the steps of the guided reading teaching sequence: setting the scene, book introduction, picture walk, reading the text, return to the text, and response. Modifications and special considerations are discussed below.

Setting the Scene

Setting the scene in transitional guided reading lessons serves the same purpose that it does in guided reading lessons. It also takes place at the same fairly quick pace as in guided reading, although with longer, more complex books it may involve additional elements. As in guided reading, the teacher tells the students the concept addressed in the book and enlists them in a conversation about what they know about that concept. Examples of concepts include friendship, envy, courage, perseverance, and other mostly affect-based ideas. In addition, books may have additional subcontexts. This conversation is critical as it establishes a framework for understanding. A graphic organizer such as a web, a character plot, or a plot map may be used if appropriate.

Book Introduction

As in guided reading, the second step of the lesson is to introduce the members of the group to the book. The teacher gives each child a copy of the book and reads the title and the author's and illustrator's names and then says something about them. If children begin with guided reading and continue with transitional guided reading, they will expect to learn something about the author and illustrator. The genre and its motifs are discussed and the protocol continues as teacher and children examine the details of the cover illustration and check the back cover, always a potential source for learning. For example, if the book contains a blurb on the back, it is read by the teacher, together by the group, or by an individual. The contents and structure of the blurb are discussed. If the book has end flaps attached to the edges of the front and back covers, these are read and discussed as well. If the book includes review statements, these are read and discussed, as is the structure of the review statements. The title page is examined, and if the book contains a dedication, foreword, or introduction, they are read and discussed. If the book has a table of contents, that's the next stop.

The book's table of contents is examined for the number of chapters or sections and the length of each. Chapter or section titles are discussed and used in making predictions. If the book is a longer picture book that is not broken into chapters, the teacher and students mark the pages where they will divide the book. Chapters break where a change in setting or action occurs. As described earlier, a sticky note is applied to the margin of the first page of a chapter. After the chapter has been read, each member of the group writes a title for it. Chapter titles are synthesis statements and reflect a literary element of character, setting, or action in fiction, or the main idea of the section in nonfiction.

Nonfiction books with access features such as table of contents, index, glossary, and the like provide additional opportunities for learning and working. Many access features are located at the back of the book, but that doesn't mean we use them last—quite the contrary. For example, after examining the table of contents and determining the beginning and ending pages of the section to be read that day, the students move to the index. With notebook or strip of adding machine tape and pencil at the ready, the students begin at the top and skim the page numbers, not the words, looking for the numbers that correspond with the pages to be read that day. As the numbers are spotted, the word and page number are recorded, thus providing a vocabulary list for the section to be read.

From the index, the students go to the glossary if one is present. Here they cross-check the list of words with entries in the glossary. Words that do not appear in the glossary are watched for during the reading. Words from the index initiate the note taking that takes place during transitional guided reading.

Picture Walk

Obviously, the picture walk takes place only if there are pictures to walk through. In longer picture books, the illustrations may offer details that add charm or humor to the story.

Illustrations in a book with only a few illustrations may serve to add to the mood or tone of the story. Or the few illustrations may serve as page fillers at the beginning or end of a chapter. Generally, only the pictures of the section that will be read during that lesson are examined. Walking through the entire book may ruin anticipation or give away the plot.

The literary elements of character, setting, and action are examined in fictional text. Character traits, development, and interaction are discussed. Likewise, aspects of setting are studied—for example, indications of the way the weather influences the action might be considered. Similarly, evidence of action is observed. Discussing evidence of each of the literary elements found in the illustrations provides opportunities to predict, interpret, infer, compare, connect, deduce, and on and on.

Illustrations are interpretations of narration and serve as visual talking points in both fiction and nonfiction text. Talking points are places in the text and illustration ripe for discussion. The teacher leads the students to an analysis of what the author is saying. In fiction, the interpretation is based on the reader's schema, so answers may vary. In nonfiction, however, the illustrations may include graphic organizers such as graphs, maps, time lines, and the like, with generally one answer.

No real reading takes place during the picture walk except for embedded print, such as thought bubbles and writing, that appears within the illustrations. Print associated with images in nonfiction texts is also read. Examples include headings, captions, labels, fact boxes, and the like.

Reading the Text and Returning to the Text

In transitional guided reading, the reading of the text and returning to it take place concurrently. Unlike in guided reading, where the whole text is read aloud by all the members of the group, in transitional guided reading the reading is done silently in the group, with the teacher observing. The segments to be read range from a paragraph to a page in length.

The teacher gives a purpose or focus for each segment. For example, the teacher might tell the students, "Read this first paragraph silently. As you read, you will learn the name of the main character and find out the setting. When you finish reading the paragraph, go back and find those two things."

The children drop their eyes and read, sweeping their fingers along the text as they read. They now have two items in their heads that serve as triggers for thinking. As they read and come across the two bits of information, the triggers are thrown and the thinking is conscious. When the teacher sees that all in the group have read the segment, perhaps putting up a thumb to indicate they are ready to discuss it, they return to the text. Together, they discuss the specifics of the segment just read, and debrief about the segment in general and specific terms. The teacher leads the discussion with a question like, "Okay, what did you find out? Tell me what this paragraph told us." The children discuss the paragraph in general to maintain a literal understanding, and then they discuss the focus points.

Assigning the children specific elements to attend to sets up a neural expectation in the brain that gives them something to focus on as they process print. Over time, the children begin to internalize these expectations and consciously attend to the details as they read. Eventually, these expectations become anticipations that cause the reader to attend fully from paragraph to paragraph.

During the reading section of the teaching sequence, the teacher might take advantage of the opportunity to have the children use study skills to locate and mark bits of information. In fiction, the students might use highlighter tape and edge tabs to mark elements such as the following:

- character names
- character traits and indicators
- evidence of setting
- plot points
- word choices
- literary language devices
- key words

In nonfiction, students might mark key words, content vocabulary, and definitions or explanations. The items that are marked during the reading indicate what will be discussed in the return to the text. Eventually, students will locate and mark bits of information while working at their seats.

A question I often hear about transitional guided reading is this: With newly fluent readers who are using denser, more complex texts, at what point does the teacher check comprehension? The truth is, I stopped checking comprehension years ago. I was tired of being constantly disappointed. I would ask the children to read a little bit of something, then ask them a few simple, literal-detail questions, and they could not answer. Why not? "Did you read it!?" I would ask them.

"Yes, yes, I did read it," they would reply. And they were not lying—they did indeed drag their eyes across the print. They might as well have said, "You didn't tell me I had to think about it." Reading the words is no guarantee that the brain will engage so that the reader will understand or even attend to what the eyes are doing.

The reason that the silent reading and return to the text happen concurrently in transitional guided reading is that this enables the teacher to ensure, rather than check, comprehension. All of the items that are set up before the read and revisited during the return to the text are teaching points. Skills and vocabulary don't get any more contextualized than this. The teaching is embedded within the specific situation of use. The teaching is exact, which increases the chances it is learned.

It was said earlier that note taking ensures the comprehension. Note taking is one of the study skills that students need to learn to use. In many places, explicit study skill instruction begins in Grade 2 with awareness events beginning in kindergarten and Grade 1 during modeled and shared reading and writing. Opportunities for note taking are more obvious in nonfiction texts, as expository writing is more straightforward; however, as stated earlier, note taking is done in fiction with the literary elements. Taking notes while reading adds a hands-on dimension to reading and serves as a link between reading and written responses.

The study skills involved in note taking include:

- locating information
- recording information
- using information

Students learn to locate information as they search for key words while working with expository features such as the table of contents, index, glossary, headings, footnotes, sidebars, callouts, and captions. Using a table of contents, students identify the beginning and ending page of each section or chapter, see the section titles as an outline of concepts, and determine the key word in each section title. Using an index, students find words from the section currently being read and copy those words and page number in a list on a strip of adding machine tape, or in a notebook. Using a glossary, students cross-check the words copied from the index with those listed in the glossary; they may use a symbol to code those index words that appear in the glossary, use a different symbol to code those words that are commonly understood, and find the words without a symbol in the body of the text. Using headings, students determine the key word in each heading, see that each heading is the main idea, and incorporate the headings and the section titles from the table of contents into an outline. Using key words, students determine the most important words in footnotes, sidebars, callouts, and captions.

Notes might be recorded using notebooks, note cards, sticky notes, or half-sheets. The rules for recording notes are few, but important. By limiting each note to no more than five words, students are prevented from copying verbatim from the text, which is an NTR (no thinking required) experience. Symbols can be used in lieu of words and they are not included in the word count. Each note is bulleted rather than using numbers or the alphabet. Numbers and letters imply a hierarchy, and that is not what notes are for—the organization of the notes comes later. The page and paragraph number from which the notes come identify each set of notes. The main idea is written on the top line. Figure 9.1 explains and illustrates the process.

Figure 9.1 How to Take Notes

	"Water, Water, Everywhere" Chapter 4. Sweaty Glass
	Page 17. ¶ 1. <u>condensation</u> • Condensation = cool water + warm air • " = liquid » gas » liquid • " = water droplets • " = foggy water on glass, webs, etc.

How to do it:

1. Name of book on top line or in top margin	
2. Number and name of the chapter beside or below the name of the book	
3. Page number	Page 17.
4. Paragraph number	¶ 1.
5. Main idea line	______________
6. First bullet and first note (< five words; symbols don't count)	* condensation = cool water + warm air
7. Next bullet and note	* " = liquid
8. Rest of notes	
9. Finally, complete the main idea line	

Figure 9.2 Sticky-Note Note

Clouds

p. 11 ¶ 1.

1. How clouds are made

↑

- Cold air rises
- Cold air + dust + water = clouds
- 3 kinds of clouds:
  - Stratus
  - Cirrus
  - Nimbus

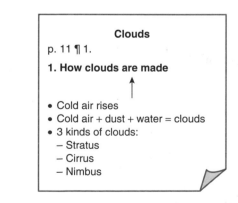

Notes can be written on sticky notes as well, as shown in Figure 9.2. The notes are attached to the margin beside the paragraph from which they come. A caution, however: sticky notes eventually have to be removed, if they don't fall out first. Once removed, they have to be put somewhere, generally into a notebook. While students enjoy the novelty of writing on sticky notes and handling them, the more practical (and economical) method is to write directly in a notebook.

In a perfect world, students would dutifully check all the information to verify that all of it is correct, ensure that all of it was indeed recorded, and perhaps even expand upon the information with questions or other bits of information that is known rather than found. This doesn't happen as often as one would hope. What can you do? Not much. At some point, the collected information needs to be manipulated—sorted, moved around, categorized, and organized according to its intended use. Which brings us to the whole reason for having students take notes in the first place: using them to express what has been learned. And that brings us to the last step of the transitional guided reading teaching sequence: responding to the text.

Responding to the Text

The last segment of the teaching sequence engages students in independent individual or small-group activities that allow them to revisit what was read during a group session and express what has been learned. The types of responses used in guided reading can be used in transitional guided reading. Box 9.1 summarizes the various types of responses.

Box 9.1   Using Information

Using the manipulated bits of information, students express understanding in written, oral, image, 3-D, or technology responses such as:

Written	Oral	Image	3-D	Technology
caption	oral report	Venn diagram	display	PowerPoint
glossary	reader's theater	graphs	book in a bag	videos
summary	acting it out	time line	museum display	photos
blurb	tapes	storyboard	diorama	
outline	interviews	plot map		
index		character map		

PRACTICES FOR TRULY FLUENT READERS

Transitional guided reading with newly fluent readers is done as long as the students need to learn how to think while reading. These children may be anywhere from second through to sixth grade. Over time, children will begin to think as they read. Once this process becomes automatic, the children are truly fluent. Unfortunately, formal reading instruction too often ends at this point. Just when children have what they need to truly appreciate literature, the instruction stops.

It is important to continue reading instruction for truly fluent readers, and there are numerous practices suitable for children at this level. Obviously, all of these practices require students to have a high level of literacy. They also require students to have a sufficient degree of maturity, since reading at this stage of development is done independently.

Maturity has two meanings here. The first is life experience. Children need to have lived long enough for their schemas to fill up with experiences that enable them to interact with all the levels of meaning that make up what they read. Without sufficient living as a field of reference, kids will miss out on much of what makes reading so good. Second, maturity means lack of goofiness. Since reading is done away from the teacher, the kids have to have the stick-to-it-iveness to complete the task in a thorough and timely manner. Nothing wrecks a lesson more than a goofy kid who didn't do the work or who acts like a jerk while in the group.

Two of the instructional practices that enable children to continue learning about reading are reader's workshops and literature circles. Variations on the Nancie Atwell model of writer's workshops and the Harvey Daniels model of literature circles will briefly be discussed here. For more information on both of these practices, refer to the Bibliography.

Children who have learned to read still need instruction in reading, and a variety of practices and experiences are appropriate through the grades.

READER'S WORKSHOP

Modeled after Atwell's writer's workshop, this practice engages the students in focused, independent reading. It is the most teacher-directed practice for fully fluent readers. Unlike the reading step in transitional guided reading, the reading here is done independently, away from the group. The teacher instigates and ensures the understanding, but the children read alone. The teaching sequence in reader's workshop allows the students to read and think independently under the direction of the teacher. Reader's workshop groups might meet with the teacher two or three times during the week.

Texts

In general, reader's workshop uses chapter books and novels. Short stories and poems may be used as well. Nonfiction texts may be used, but a practice better suited to nonfiction is reciprocal teaching. (For more information on this approach, see the source by Palinscar and Brown cited in the Bibliography.)

Groups

With reader's workshop, the groups are no longer homogeneous in the traditional sense of the term. The very nature of being able to read and think while reading renders truly fluent readers homogeneous. Therefore, groups for reader's workshop may be built around personal interests, social tendencies, genre, or author. Students at this stage of development might indicate an interest in being in one group or another. Group size might increase to seven or eight members.

An important guideline for reader's workshop is that the groups remain intact during the reading of a story or novel—students may not opt out of a group once a text has been selected. No one is allowed to decide, "This story just isn't doing it for me." With the longer texts used at this level, this guideline helps children learn to stick with a text and give it a chance before tossing it away for something else.

Once a group's text is finished, the children might read independently in other texts for a few days or even a week while another reader's workshop group finishes up with their text. The two groups might then commingle and form two new groups.

Teaching Sequence

The teaching sequence used for reader's workshop shares much common ground with the sequence used in transitional guided reading. The teacher leads students in their reading and understanding of increasingly challenging text, while preparing them for the structure they will encounter later when they are ready for literature circles. Like the guided reading teaching sequence, the reader's workshop sequence consists of five steps. These steps—setting the scene, the mini-lesson, the read, the segment debrief, and the focus debrief—are discussed below.

Setting the Scene

Setting the scene with a new book in reader's workshop is similar to setting the scene in guided reading and transitional guided reading. Chapter 8 describes each step of the teaching sequence.

The Mini-Lesson

Once the teacher has given the overview, he or she orchestrates the reading. This means the teacher determines how much material (one or more chapters or a certain number of pages) will be read by what date. The teacher establishes a focus, an objective, and a purpose for the segment, just as in transitional guided reading. The difference is that the focus is for a much longer bit of text. The focus might deal with the concept, some aspect of language, or an element of the writer's craft such as literary language, structure, stylistic devices, plot point, dimension of setting, character trait or indicator, or character development.

The mini-lesson separates reader's workshop from other instructional practices. It centers around the element of craft the teacher determines the focus to be for the current segment of reading. The mini-lesson serves a number of purposes. For example, it might prepare students to learn the focus concept, skill, or vocabulary; it might provide a review for an element the students already know; or it might give them practice. The mini-lesson certainly can serve as an assessment of the learning.

The operative word here is "mini." The lesson lasts only about five to seven minutes. The specifics of the lesson are embedded within the text. The teacher gives the students some kind of responsibility for interacting with the focus while reading independently. The responsibility might involve locating and marking examples, rewriting an example, annotating what is read, or developing a character trait map or plot map.

Reading

Before dismissing the group, the teacher tells the students when they must have the reading done and their responsibilities completed. Generally, the members depart the group with lesson and responsibilities in hand and mind, and head back to their seats to work. Reading the text can happen during the school day or as homework.

Debriefing

After the students read the segment, they return with their texts and notes for the next group meeting. The teacher debriefs with the group on the whole segment and then on the specific focus points that made up the mini-lesson. An informal assessment of text understanding as well as focus understanding is done. This assessment informs the teacher's decision making for the immediate lesson. Depending on the level of understanding, the teacher may decide to have students reread and review the current selection before going on to the next, or may decide to have students continue on with the next segment of the book. The particulars of the instructional routine are always decided on the basis of the amount and quality of the learning the students demonstrate.

LITERATURE CIRCLES

Literature circles, which pick up where reader's workshop leaves off, continue to shift more and different types of responsibility onto the reader. Literature circles are another form of small-group reading practice using chapter books and novels. (For nonfiction, the appropriate practice is reciprocal teaching.) The goal is to develop open, natural conversations about books while focusing on the specific elements of the content and the writer's craft. The focus in literature circles comes from the different roles the readers assume. It is these roles and their associated responsibilities that separate literature circles from other instructional practices. They involve readers in formal, and eventually informal, discussions of various aspects of the text.

As in reader's workshop, groups are organized around interest, genre, author, or social aspects rather than need. The specific roles included in the circle determine the number of participants. A literature circle might have as many as eight or nine members. The groups may meet two or three times each week. The group selects the text, generally from an array predetermined by the teacher, and the members of the group orchestrate the reading. That is, the students determine how much will be read by when. They learned how to do this in reader's workshop and so are able to do this on their own now. As before, the reading is done alone, away from the group.

Roles and Responsibilities

When preparing a group of students for participation in literature circles, the teacher needs to train them in the various roles and responsibilities. Some possible roles are as follows:

- **The Discussion Director** serves as the boss of the group. This child initiates the discussion, keeps it going, and determines who reports next.
- **The Vocabulary Master** looks out for words and phrases he or she decides the group should discuss. This child provides definitions or explanations of words.
- **The Scene Setter** gives an update on the settings for each segment. This child describes all the dimensions of each setting, including weather, time of day, week, month, or year.
- **The Character Captain** reports on the current status of major and minor characters, discusses characters new to the segment, and mentions characters that are not in the current segment. This child discusses character interplay and feelings.
- **The Passage Picker** watches for interesting or memorable bits of text. This child reports on literary language such as figures of speech, similes and metaphors, colloquialisms, and so on.
- **The Illustrator** represents the segment via illustration. This child might construct a time line that gets passed along to illustrators who follow, or might contribute a frame to a storyboard.
- **The Connector** relates the character, setting, and plot within the current segment of text to other texts, current events, and his or her own life.
- **The Researcher** investigates and reports on elements within the text. For example, if the story takes place in France, this child probes details of France.

Each role targets one aspect of the text, motif, or writer's craft. Different roles have different kinds of recording forms that allow the students to take notes that will aid in the discussion following the reading.

The Two Phases of Literature Circles

Phase One of the training for literature circles has the teacher directing the learning of each role. The teacher might teach each role to the members of the group, one role at a time. The children learn how to read with one role in mind, learn to use the recording forms, and learn to participate in the discussion within that role. After the children have learned the basics of each role, they move into individual roles. It is important to remember that the teacher has a major responsibility for ensuring that each child understands and can participate fully in each role. Therefore, during this training phase, the teacher is a full-time participant.

Over time, the teacher becomes less and less a member of the group. Overt teaching and modeling shift to coaching and observing, as the children take on greater and greater responsibilities. Eventually, the teacher becomes a nonmember of the group.

Phase Two begins when the children are able to select text, orchestrate the reading, read and prepare to take part, participate fully in their rotating roles, and conduct the discussion sessions without supervision. Ultimately, the roles dissolve and the children read and discuss thoughtfully. When this occurs, the children are at the brink of proficiency, the highest level of literacy development.

SUMMARY

Well, that's it, teaching reading and comprehending from beginning to end. But it's not really the end because learning never ends. We are proof of that fact. If learning didn't continue, we wouldn't have made it this far.

So what's next? I suppose one of the goobers we teach every day will someday have an original thought and you and I will be reading about it—probably on some front-projection plasma thingy.

I must say, it has been a hoot talking with you about teaching children to read. I had a great time. How about it, was it good for you? Bye.

Glossary

Ability group: the type of group used in traditional small-group reading instruction. Generally consists of five to eight children who share a similar range of facility with reading text. The makeup of these groups rarely changes over the course of a year.

Aliteracy: a condition seen in newly fluent readers who can read, but choose not to.

Bottom power: the capacity a reader has to sit and participate in an event that is not his or her own idea, such as a guided reading lesson.

Challenges: features in a book that cause a reader to slow down and work.

Coaching statements: a type of teacher talk; positive statements by the teacher that guide a reader's thinking by reminding the reader what he or she knows.

Comprehending skills: mental actions taken by a reader to connect the author's words with meaning in the reader's head, with meaning in other texts, or with meaning in the world at large.

Concept: what the children will learn about from reading the text; the theme in fiction, the content in nonfiction.

Content vocabulary: words directly related to the concept in a text.

Early: the third stage of literacy development; follows the preemergent and emergent stages. Early readers have learned to use strategies and are beginning to self-monitor.

Elements of craft: the specific aspects of literature that writers use, such as literary elements, languages, devices, and structures.

Emergent: the second stage of literacy development; follows the preemergent stage. Emergent readers have control of the six literacy behaviors needed to benefit from the first type of formal small-group reading instruction, guided reading. This is the stage of development where strategies are learned.

False positive readers: newly fluent readers who can read a wide range of material but do not have a clue about what they read.

Familiar text: instructional text for which readers have a talking understanding of the concept, can read or work through 90–95 percent of the words, and can use 90–95 percent of the skills.

Fluency: a multidimensional facet of reading, made up of comprehending what is read, reading with self-monitoring and accuracy, reading smoothly with expression, and reading increasingly challenging text.

Fresh text: instructional text that the members of the group have not read, seen, or heard.

Guided reading: one of several types of small-group practices for reading instruction. It is the instructional practice for emergent and early readers for the purpose of teaching reading strategies.

Homogeneous group: the ideal type of group formation for guided reading and transitional guided reading. Four, five, or six children who know, use, and need to learn the same concepts, skills, and vocabulary and who process text using the same strategies; four to six children who operate on text as though they were one child. Individuals may move out of a group and into another as they cease to be homogeneous with a group.

Instructional practice: any type of small-group interaction between learners and an informed other, such as a teacher, for the purpose of connecting bits of new concept, skill, vocabulary, or strategy information to existing concept, skill, vocabulary, or strategy information. Features include the use of specifically selected texts and/or materials; direct, explicit instruction; guided practice; and monitoring by the teacher.

Instructional text: a text, generally a leveled book or longer picture book for use in any instructional practice, with a ratio of 90–95 percent supports to 5–10 percent challenges for fiction; 93–97 percent supports for nonfiction.

Leveled books: books of 8–32 pages written specifically for reading instruction, leveled according to ratios of supports to challenges.

Literary elements: the characters, setting, and plot points in a fictional text.

Literature circles: one of several instructional practices for truly fluent readers using chapter books and novels. Roles and responsibilities distinguish this practice from others.

Little books: eight- to twelve-page books published by educational publishers for use in guided reading lessons with emergent and early readers.

Longer picture books: twelve- to twenty-four-page books published by educational publishers for use in transitional guided reading lessons with newly fluent readers.

Metacognition: knowing what one knows; a reader needs to metacognize to recognize the specific strategies used to make meaning.

Metacognitive teacher talk: coaching statements, questions, and prompts given by a teacher to the readers during and after the reading to make strategy use obvious to the readers so the strategies will be used again.

Newly fluent: the fourth stage of literacy development; follows the preemergent, emergent, and early stages. Newly fluent readers need transitional guided reading. These readers are at risk for becoming aliterate or false positive readers.

Phonemic awareness: the ability to distinguish smaller and smaller units of sound within a linguistic stream.

Preemergent: the first stage of literacy development along the continuum where readers learn how a language works. Six literacy behaviors needed to benefit from guided reading are developed during this stage of development: concepts of print, letter names, the sounds given to letters and letter combinations, phonemic awareness, sight words, and fifteen minutes of "bottom power."

Proficiency: the highest stage of literacy development. Readers at this stage of development are addicted to print and have an internal, self-fulfilling need to read.

Prompts: a type of teacher talk; statements that tell a reader what to do with a source of information.

Questions: a type of teacher talk; interrogatives used by a teacher to guide readers to self-monitor, or to guide them toward a source of information.

Reader's workshop: one of several instructional practices for truly fluent readers that use chapter books and novels. The teacher orchestrates the reading with a mini-lesson and the children read the predetermined segment of text independently.

Responses: verbal, image, written, or three-dimensional actions, and technology taken by the reader to express understanding while revisiting the concepts, skills, and vocabulary found in the text.

Self-monitoring: the awareness a reader has that the meaning has broken down. It is the first layer of comprehending.

Shared reading: a read-together interaction between a whole or small group and a teacher using an enlarged text.

Sight words: high-utility, automatically recognized words, including environmental words.

Skills: isolated bits that connect with other isolated bits to form a whole. Literacy skills include listening, speaking, reading, writing, observing, and representing. Reading and writing skills include phonics, grammar, and the conventions of print such as punctuation, indenting, capitalization, and spelling. Study and comprehending are two additional types of skills.

Sources of information: ideas, words, word meanings, grammar, contexts, and phonics a reader uses to problem solve through a text.

Strategies: the in-the-head problem-solving actions a reader takes to puzzle out words. Conscious decisions made by the reader to use one or more sources of information to make and maintain the meaning.

Study skills: actions taken by a reader to locate, record, retrieve, manipulate, and use information.

Supports: features of text that render the book appropriate for instruction. Fiction instructional texts should be 90–95 percent supportive; nonfiction texts should be 93–97 percent supportive.

Talking points: places within the text or illustration that allow for discussion of various types of comprehending, such as inferring, predicting, comparing, and so on.

Teacher talk: specific coaching statements, questions, and prompts that guide readers' mental actions before and during reading for inquiry, and during and after the reading for metacognition.

Teaching points: skills and vocabulary within a text that are unfamiliar to the readers and form the instructional focus of the lesson.

Transitional guided reading: one of several small-group instructional practices for reading instruction. The instructional practice for newly fluent readers, it focuses on comprehending the text as it is read.

Truly fluent: the fifth stage of literacy development; follows the preemergent, emergent, early, and newly fluent stages. Truly fluent readers can read, and they understand what they read. Instructional tactics for these readers include reader's workshop, literature circles, book clubs, reciprocal teaching, and various instructional practices that are designed to take children higher in their thinking and deeper in their understanding.

Workable words: words other than sight words; words that can be figured out through various strategies.

Resource List

ORGANIZATIONS

Association for Supervision and Curriculum Development
1703 North Beauregard Street
Alexandria, VA 22311–1714
http://www.ascd.org

International Reading Association
800 Barksdale Road
P.O. Box 8139
Newark, DE 19714–8139
http://www.ira.org

National Council of Teachers of English
1111 Kenyon Road
Urbana, IL 61801
http://www.ncte.org

National Staff Development Council
P.O. Box 240
Oxford, OH 45056
http://www.nsdc.org

Reading Recovery® Council of North America
1929 Kenny Road, Suite 100
Columbus, OH 43210–1069
http://www.readingrecovery.org

PUBLISHERS OF GUIDED READING MATERIALS

Capstone Press
http://www.capstone-press.com
http://www.newbridgeonline.com

Steck-Vaughn Company
http://www.steck-vaughn.com

Rigby Education
http://www.rigby.com

Bibliography

Boushey, G., & Moser, J. (2006). *The daily five: Fostering literacy independence in the elementary grades*. Portland, ME: Stenhouse.

Burke, T., & Hartzold, K. (2007). *One lesson, all levels, any text.* Peterborough, NH: Crystal Springs.

Burns, B. (2001). *Guided reading: A how-to for all grades.* Thousand oaks, CA: Corwin Press.

Daniels, H. (2002). *Literature circles: Voice and choice in book clubs and reading groups.* Portland, ME: Stenhouse Publishers.

Denton, P. (2007). *The power of our words: Teacher language that helps children learn.* Turner's Falls, MA: Northeast Foundation for Children.

Diller, D. (2007). *Making the most of small groups: Differentiation for all.* Portland, ME: Stenhouse.

Fountas, I. C., & Pinnell, G. S. (2005). *Leveled books, K–8: Matching texts to readers for effective teaching.* Portsmouth, NH: Heinemann.

Fountas, I. C., & Pinnell, G. S. (2005). *The Fountas and Pinnell leveled book list, K–8, 2006–2008 edition.* Portsmouth, NH: Heinemann.

Hoyt, L. (2004). *Spotlight on comprehension: Building a literacy of thoughtfulness.* Portsmouth, NH: Heinemann.

Jamison Rog, L. (2003). *Guided reading basics: Organizing, managing, and implementing a balanced literacy program in K–3.* Portland, ME: Stenhouse Publishers.

Johnston, P. H. (2004). *Choice words: How our language affects children's learning.* Portland, ME: Stenhouse.

Keene, E. O., & Zimmermann, S. (2007). *Mosaic of thought, 2nd ed.: The power of comprehension strategey instruction.* Portsmouth, NH: Heinemann.

Mere, C. (2005). *More than guided reading: Finding the right intructional mix, K–3.* Portland, ME: Stenhouse Publishers.

Miller, D. (2002). *Reading with meaning: Teaching comprehension in the primary grades.* Portland, ME: Stenhouse.

Oczkus, L. D. (2003). *Reciprocal teaching at work: Strategies for improving reading comprehension.* Newark, DE: International Reading Association.

Palinscar, A. S. & Brown, A.L. (1984). Reciprocal teaching of comprehension fostering and monitoring activities. *Cognition and Instruction,* 1, 117–175

Pinnell, G. S., & Fountas, I. C. (2007). *The continuum of literacy learning, Grades K–2: A guide to teaching.* Portsmouth, NH: Heinemann.

Raphael, T. E., et al. (2004). *Book clubs plus! A literacy framework for the primary grades.* Lawrence, MA: Small Planet Communications.

Reutzel, D. R., & Cooter, R. B., Jr. (2008). *Teaching children to read: The teacher makes the difference, 5th ed.* Upper Saddle River, NJ: Pearson.

Routman, R. (2002). *Reading essentials: The specifics you need to teach reading well.* Portsmouth, NH: Heinemann.

Saunders-Smith, G. (2005). *The ultimate small group reading how-to book.* Chicago, IL : Zephyr Press.

Tomlinson, C. A. (2004). *How to differentiate instruction in mixed ability classrooms, 2nd ed.* Alexandria, VA: ASCD.

Witherelle, N. L. (2007). *The guided reading classroom: How to keep all students working constructively.* Portsmouth, NH: Heinemann.